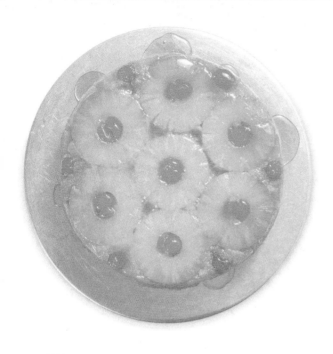

SIMPLY THE BEST
TWIST & MIX RECIPES

MARIAN GETZ

INTRODUCTION BY WOLFGANG PUCK

AS I LEARNED LONG AGO, ALONGS
AND GRANDMOTHER, YOU SHOULD
LOTS OF LOVE INTO EVERYTHING YO
IS CERTAINLY EVIDENT IN THIS COC

Wolfgang Puck

The modern tools we have in the kitchen, whether in the restaurant or at home, are expected to be able to do more than one thing. The Twist & Mix is a versatile appliance with exchangeable attachments and adjustable positions that makes it indispensable in the kitchen. You can do anything from mixing cookie dough, emulsifying egg whites or creating the perfect smoothie or thick milkshake.

When I asked Marian to write the cookbook for the Twist & Mix, I knew she would rise to the occasion. Her experience as a pastry chef, wife, mother, and now grandmother allowed Marian to put together a cookbook with a wide variety of recipes that I'm sure you will use for years to come.

A student of cooking is probably one of the best ways to describe Marian. She is always looking for something new, something fresh, something local, something seasonal. Her culinary knowledge combined with her passion for cooking is second to none. The recipes that Marian has written for this cookbook will motivate you to be more creative in the kitchen.

INTRODUCTION BY WOLFGANG PUCK

RECIPES

TABLE OF CONTENTS

TWIST & MIX TIPS

BAKING

Baking can be intimidating but it can be very rewarding and easy to do if you follow these main steps:

1 Measure ingredients accurately.
2 Use good measuring equipment such as metal cups and spoons.
3 Know your oven and whether it is accurately calibrated.
4 Use a timer (such as your smart phone you can carry with you if you step away from the kitchen) to monitor baking time accurately.

BE ORGANIZED

Read through the entire recipe once then gather all the ingredients prior to baking. This will help you get a better overview of the recipe and keep you organized.

MEASURING

Measuring ingredients accurately is critical to achieving the baking results you desire. Use glass measuring cups with measuring marks to measure liquid ingredients. To use them, place them on the counter and tilt your head down to look directly at the measuring line you are aiming for while filling the cup. This is the only way to be truly accurate with liquid measuring. Use metal measuring cups and the dip and sweep method to measure dry ingredients. Dip the cup into the ingredient, such as flour or sugar, then overfill it slightly. Use the flat side of a butter knife to sweep off the excess until it is perfectly level with the rim. This is not possible with a glass measuring cup because the measuring lines are recessed below the rim. I also recommend using narrow measuring spoons as they are small enough to fit into the neck of a spice jar. It is also best to measure ingredients ahead of time so you don't get distracted. You can also use a digital kitchen scale for the easiest and most accurate measuring of all. It is not widely used in North America but is gaining in popularity and yields the most accurate result.

MEASURING IN PILES

Try to keep the dry ingredients as separate as possible when adding to a mixing bowl. For example, add the flour then add the sugar in a separate pile inside the bowl. If the recipe calls for 2 teaspoons of baking powder, drop those ingredients into two separate little piles next to each other then repeat with the rest of the ingredients. By measuring in piles, you will be able to read over the ingredients you already added to the mixing bowl in case you lose track or get distracted. Incorrect measuring is the most common baking mistake that is easily overlooked so applying this measuring method will help you achieve better baking success in the kitchen.

USE CAUTION

Use caution when dealing with hot baked goods as they can produce burns if not handled correctly. Always use oven mitts or potholders when handling hot items and protect your countertop with a trivet or other heat-proof stand if necessary.

TESTING FOR DONENESS

To test cakes for doneness, insert a toothpick or bamboo skewer off-center. It should generally come out with just a few moist crumbs clinging to it. For custards, insert a knife off-center, it should come out clean. For breads, bake until the internal temperature registers 200°F on a thermometer. For cookies, pizzas and pastries, look for slight puffing and a brown color. Correct oil temperature while frying is also important to the outcome of the fried food so always use caution and a deep frying thermometer to monitor oil temperature.

ROTATING BAKING SHEETS

Rotating baking sheets from top to bottom and turning the trays 180 degrees in the middle of the baking cycle helps to ensure even baking. This is true in conventional and convection baking.

PREVENT STICKING

Use parchment paper, nonstick cooking spray or silicone coated aluminum foil to prevent sticking and help clean up your bakeware faster.

TESTING YOUR OVEN FOR ACCURATE TEMPERATURE

The recipes in the cookbook assume that your oven's temperature is accurate. Most ovens are not accurate and require you to compensate for the difference. To test your oven, place an inexpensive oven thermometer in the center of your oven on the center rack and let the oven heat to 350°F. After 30 minutes, check the temperature shown on your oven thermometer. Make note of the difference and adjust your temperature accordingly each time you bake.

THERMOMETERS

An instant-read thermometer is used throughout the book to tell if your baked goods or meats are done. You can also use it to check if the oil for frying reaches the correct temperature if you don't have a deep frying thermometer. To test foods for doneness, insert into the thickest part of the food.

BEATER ATTACHMENT

Think of the beater attachment as your all purpose tool. If in doubt, reach for the beater. It is great at thoroughly mixing ingredients together faster and better than you could possibly do with a wooden spoon. A boxed cake mix made by hand using a wooden spoon will be noticeably denser, lumpier and lower in height than using the Twist & Mix fitted with the beater. This is because the Twist & Mix operates at a steady speed and makes it effortless to use. The beater is mostly used for batters in this cookbook.

WIRE WHISK ATTACHMENT

The wire whisk attachment is best used for mixtures that are very thin in texture where you want to incorporate a lot of air such as egg whites, skim milk or cream. The whisk is never used for thick or heavy batters.

DRINK MIXER ATTACHMENT

This attachment is great at making homemade milkshakes, emulsifying recipes and making protein shakes. To use it, push the spindle to the bottom of the container and always start on LOW speed before increasing speed to HIGH to prevent potential splashing. This is true for all of the attachments.

PANTRY TIPS

Being prepared to cook or bake the recipes in this book, or any recipe for that matter, is one of the keys to success in the kitchen. Your pantry must be stocked with the basics. We all know how frustrating it can be when you go to the cupboard and what you need is not there. This list includes some of the ingredients you will find in this book and some that we feel are important to always have on hand.

PERISHABLES	SPICES	DRY GOODS
ONIONS	KOSHER SALT	VARIETY OF FLOURS
GARLIC	FRESH PEPPERCORNS	YEAST
TOMATOES	BAY LEAVES	WHITE AND BROWN SUGARS
CARROTS	SAGE	SUGAR SUBSTITUTE
CELERY	OREGANO	BAKING SODA
GINGER	THYME	BAKING POWDER
BELL PEPPERS	CHILI FLAKES	CORN STARCH
WHITE POTATOES	CUMIN SEEDS	GROUND CINNAMON
SWEET POTATOES	CURRY POWDER	HONEY AND VANILLA
SQUASHES	ONION POWDER	EXTRACTS/FLAVORINGS
CITRUS	GARLIC POWDER	AGAVE SYRUP
APPLES	DRY MUSTARD	CANNED TOMATOES
BANANAS	GROUND CINNAMON	CANNED VEGETABLES/BEANS
LETTUCE	NUTMEG	DRIED CHILLIES
SPINACH	CLOVES	PASTA
FRESH HERBS	CHILI POWDER	STOCKS
GREEN ONIONS		POWDERED BOUILLON
MILK		KETCHUP
CREAM CHEESE		MUSTARD
PARMESAN CHEESE		OILS
YOGURT		VINEGAR
OTHER CHEESES YOU LIKE		GROUND GINGER
FROZEN FRUIT/VEGETABLES		PICKLES

It is not necessary to have all the items listed at all times. However, if you are feeling creative, adventurous or just following a recipe, it's great to have a good selection in the kitchen.

CHOCOLATE FUDGE
MILKSHAKE

Makes 1 serving

Ingredients:

4 big scoops vanilla ice cream
1/4 cup chocolate fudge + more for serving
1/2 cup whole milk

Method:

1. Place all ingredients into a tall glass.
2. Attach the Drink Mixer to the Twist & Mix then set to the Drink Mixer Position.
3. Mix on LOW for a few seconds then increase speed to HIGH and mix until smooth.
4. Put a spoonful of fudge into the bottom of a drinking glass then pour in milkshake and top with additional fudge before serving.

EASY BAKED
ALASKA

Makes 4-6 servings

Ingredients:

1 store-bought pound cake, sliced

4 big scoops any flavor sorbet or ice cream

6 large egg whites

1/4 teaspoon cream of tartar

2/3 cup granulated sugar

Method:

1. *Arrange pound cake slices into a rectangle on a heat-proof serving platter.*
2. *Place ice cream scoops on top of pound cake then place entire platter in the freezer while you make the meringue.*
3. *If you do not have a blowtorch, preheat the broiler to high.*
4. *To make the meringue, place the egg whites into a large, clean metal mixing bowl.*
5. *Attach the Wire Whisk to the Twist & Mix then set to the Whisk Position.*
6. *Whisk eggs on HIGH for 20 seconds or until foamy then add the cream of tartar and mix for an additional 30 seconds.*
7. *Slowly add the sugar and continue to mix on HIGH for 3-4 minutes or until stiff peaks form.*
8. *Remove platter from freezer then pile meringue over ice cream and pound cake until covered.*
9. *Brown meringue using a blowtorch or broil for 1-2 minutes or until brown.*
10. *Serve immediately.*

LEMON CURD

Makes about 3 cups

Ingredients:

3/4 cup granulated sugar

2 tablespoons lemon zest

3/4 cup fresh lemon juice

6 large egg yolks

3/4 cup unsalted butter, cubed

Method:

1. Fashion a double boiler by setting a metal or heat-proof glass bowl over a saucepan so that it nests comfortably. Bring 2 inches of water to a simmer over medium heat (the bottom of the bowl should not touch the water).
2. Place the sugar, lemon zest, lemon juice and egg yolks into the metal or glass bowl.
3. Attach the Wire Whisk to the Twist & Mix then set to the Whisk Position.
4. Whisk briefly every 45 seconds on LOW for 5-8 minutes or until mixture is too hot to touch and has thickened significantly.
5. Remove from heat and let cool for 5 minutes.
6. Whisk in the butter on LOW until melted and smooth.
7. Lemon curd can be stored in an airtight container in the refrigerator for up to 2 weeks or freeze for up to 2 months.

CHOCOLATE CHIP
COOKIES

Makes about 24 cookies

Ingredients:

1 cup unsalted butter, softened

1 cup granulated sugar

1/2 cup light brown sugar, packed

2 large eggs

2 teaspoons vanilla extract

1 teaspoon kosher salt

1 teaspoon baking soda

2 cups all purpose flour

2 cups semi-sweet chocolate chips

Method:

1. *Preheat oven to 325°F.*
2. *Place the butter into a large mixing bowl.*
3. *Attach the Beater to the Twist & Mix then set to the Hand Mixer Position.*
4. *Cream the butter then add the sugars, eggs, vanilla, salt, baking soda, flour and chocolate chips, being sure to mix well after each ingredient is added.*
5. *Drop the dough by 2 tablespoons onto foil or parchment lined cookie sheets.*
6. *Bake for 12-15 minutes or until cookies are golden in color (rotate cookie sheets 180 degrees halfway through baking time).*
7. *Remove immediately.*

TIP

If you like chewy cookies, as soon as you remove a cookie sheet from the oven, grasp it with potholders and rap the pan flat down on the counter twice. This will deflate the cookies slightly and greatly improve the chewy texture.

BACON MEATLOAF

Makes 4-6 servings

Ingredients:

1 pound ground beef

1 large egg

1/2 cup soda crackers, crumbled

1/4 cup bottled BBQ sauce + more for serving

1/4 cup ketchup

2 tablespoons whole milk

1 small yellow onion, chopped

1 teaspoon dried sage

2 teaspoons kosher salt or to taste

1/2 teaspoon freshly cracked black pepper

8 bacon slices, chopped

Method:

1. Preheat oven to 350°F.
2. Place all ingredients into a mixing bowl.
3. Attach the Beater to the Twist & Mix then set to the Hand Mixer Position.
4. Mix for 1 minute or until combined; do not over mix.
5. Pour mixture onto a sheet pan lined with aluminum foil then form into an oval shape.
6. Bake for 40-45 minutes or until internal temperature reaches 165°F on a thermometer.
7. Remove loaf, brush with additional BBQ sauce, garnish as desired and serve.

EASY
GUACAMOLE

Makes 4-5 servings

Ingredients:

2 ripe avocados, pits removed

Juice of 1 lime

1 small jalapeño pepper, minced

1/2 small white onion, minced

1/2 cup grape tomatoes, diced

A handful of fresh cilantro, chopped

Kosher salt to taste

Method:

1. *Place all ingredients into a mixing bowl.*
2. *Attach the Beater to the Twist & Mix then set to the Hand Mixer Position.*
3. *Mix on LOW then increase speed to HIGH and mix for 1-2 minutes or until chunky.*
4. *Scrape into a serving dish and serve as desired.*

MASHED
POTATOES

Makes 6 servings

Ingredients:

4 pounds Yukon Gold potatoes, peeled and chunked
Kosher salt and fresh pepper to taste
1/4 cup unsalted butter
1 1/4 cups half & half + more if needed

Method:

1. *Place potatoes and some salt into a large pot then add cold water until potatoes are covered by 1-inch of water.*
2. *Bring to a boil over high heat then reduce heat to a simmer.*
3. *Let potatoes simmer for 15 minutes or until tender.*
4. *Drain potatoes thoroughly.*
5. *Season with additional salt and pepper then add the butter to the potatoes.*
6. *Attach the Beater to the Twist & Mix then set to the Hand Mixer Position.*
7. *Mix on LOW then increase speed to HIGH and mix while adding the half & half.*
8. *Mix as quickly as possible for as short of time as possible until desired texture is achieved.*
9. *Garnish as desired and serve hot.*

TIP

Do not over mix the potatoes or they will become gluey instead of fluffy.

FRITTATA
BAKE

Makes 4-6 servings

Ingredients:

1 tablespoon olive oil

1 pound small potatoes, cooked

1 medium yellow onion, sliced

1/2 pound asparagus, sliced

1 cup grape tomatoes

1/2 cup black olives

1 cup ricotta cheese

8 large eggs

1/2 cup Parmesan cheese, grated

Kosher salt and fresh pepper to taste

Method:

1. Preheat oven to 350°F and brush olive oil over a 10-inch skillet or cake pan.
2. Scatter the potatoes, onions, asparagus, tomatoes and olives over the oiled skillet or pan.
3. Place remaining ingredients into a mixing bowl.
4. Attach the Wire Whisk to the Twist & Mix then set to the Whisk Position.
5. Whisk on HIGH for 2 minutes or until smooth.
6. Pour mixture over the skillet/pan contents then place in the oven.
7. Bake for 30-40 minutes or until very brown and puffed.
8. Remove, garnish as desired and serve.

BEST GERMAN CHOCOLATE
BROWNIES

Makes 9 brownies

Ingredients:

For the Brownies:

1/2 cup unsalted butter

6 ounces semi-sweet chocolate pieces

2 large eggs

3/4 cup granulated sugar

2 teaspoons vanilla extract

1/2 cup pecan pieces, toasted

3/4 cup all purpose flour

Pinch of kosher salt

For the Topping:

1/2 cup heavy cream

2 tablespoons corn starch

1/4 cup unsalted butter

2 large egg yolks

1/2 cup dark brown sugar, packed

1/4 teaspoon kosher salt

1 teaspoon vanilla extract

3/4 cup shredded coconut, toasted

1/2 cup pecan pieces, toasted

TIP

To toast the pecans and coconut, spread them separately on sheet pans then bake at 350°F for 10-15 minutes or until brown and fragrant. The coconut will brown fastest because it contains sugar.

RECIPES

Method:

1. Preheat oven to 350°F.
2. Line an 8x8-inch pan with aluminum foil then apply nonstick cooking spray.
3. Place the butter and chocolate into a large microwave-safe bowl then place in the microwave for 2 minutes; stir then microwave for an additional 1 minute or until all chocolate is melted.
4. Attach the Beater to the Twist & Mix then set to the Hand Mixer Position.
5. Add the eggs to the chocolate mixture and mix on LOW for 1 minute.
6. Add remaining brownie ingredients and mix on LOW just until no flour spots remain.
7. Scrape into prepared pan then bake for 20-25 minutes or until just set; remove and let cool.
8. For the topping, place the cream, corn starch, butter, egg yolks and sugar into a sauce pan.
9. Place pan over medium-low heat and mix on LOW for 5 minutes or just until mixture thickens and a few bubbles erupt on surface; do not over cook or mixture will scramble.
10. Remove from heat then add remaining topping ingredients and mix on LOW to incorporate.
11. Scrape topping from sauce pan onto brownies and spread evenly.
12. Let cool for a minimum of 30 minutes then garnish as desired and serve.

BUFFALO CHICKEN
DIP

Makes 6-8 servings

Ingredients:

1/2 cup Parmesan cheese, grated

1 package (8 ounces) cream cheese, softened

1 bunch green onions, sliced

1/4 cup whole milk

1/2 cup bottled wing sauce + more for serving

Kosher salt and fresh pepper to taste

2 cups leftover rotisserie chicken, chopped

Blue cheese, for topping

Canned French fried onions, for topping

Celery and potato chips, for dipping

RECIPES

Method:

1. Place Parmesan, cream cheese, green onions, milk and wing sauce into a mixing bowl.
2. Attach the Beater to the Twist & Mix then set to the Hand Mixer Position.
3. Mix on LOW for a few seconds then increase speed to HIGH and mix for 1-2 minutes or until smooth.
4. Add salt, pepper and chicken to the bowl then mix on LOW just until blended.
5. Scrape into a serving dish then drizzle with additional wing sauce.
6. Scatter some blue cheese and French fried onions over the top.
7. Garnish as desired then serve with celery and potato chips for dipping.

TIP

To turn this into a hot dip, bake at 350°F for 25-30 minutes or until brown and bubbly.

EASY
PANCAKES

Makes about 12 pancakes

Ingredients:

1/3 cup sour cream

2 cups buttermilk

3 large eggs

2 cups unbleached all purpose flour

1 teaspoon kosher salt

2 tablespoons granulated sugar

1/2 teaspoon baking soda

1 teaspoon baking powder

Butter and syrup, for serving

Method:

1. *Preheat an electric griddle to 350°F or a pan over medium heat.*
2. *Place sour cream, buttermilk and eggs into a large mixing bowl.*
3. *Attach the Beater to the Twist & Mix then set to the Hand Mixer Position.*
4. *Mix on LOW for a few seconds then increase speed to HIGH for 30 seconds.*
5. *Add remaining ingredients, except butter and syrup, then mix on LOW to incorporate; do not over mix and allow some lumps to remain which will allow for fluffy pancakes.*
6. *Let batter rest for 5 minutes.*
7. *Ladle batter onto griddle/into pan and cook for about 2 minutes on each side.*
8. *Remove and repeat with remaining batter to make additional pancakes.*
9. *Garnish as desired and serve hot with butter and syrup.*

VANILLA CUPCAKES

Makes 24 cupcakes

Ingredients:

3 cups cake flour

1 1/2 cups all purpose flour

3/4 teaspoon baking soda

2 1/4 teaspoons baking powder

2 teaspoons kosher salt

1 cup + 2 tablespoons unsalted butter

2 1/3 cups granulated sugar

5 large eggs

3 large egg yolks

2 cups buttermilk

1 tablespoon vanilla extract

7 Minute Frosting (see page 40)

Method:

1. Preheat oven to 350°F and prepare a cupcake pan with papers; set aside.
2. In a bowl, sift together the flours, baking soda, baking powder and salt.
3. Place the butter and sugar into a separate mixing bowl.
4. Attach the Beater to the Twist & Mix then set to the Hand Mixer Position.
5. Mix the butter-sugar mixture on LOW for 1-2 minutes.
6. While mixing on LOW, add the eggs, one at a time, then add the egg yolks.
7. While continuing to mix on LOW, add the flour mixture and buttermilk in batches, alternating between the two until incorporated.
8. Add the vanilla extract and mix on LOW to incorporate.
9. Using an ice cream scoop, fill cupcake papers with batter until each is 3/4 full.
10. Bake for 20 minutes or until golden brown.
11. Let cool before icing with the 7 Minute Frosting.

TIP

Fill with Lemon Curd from page 12 for a nice surprise.

VIETNAMESE COFFEE LATTE

Makes 1 serving

Ingredients:

1/2 cup fat-free milk, cold
3 tablespoons sweetened condensed milk
2/3 cup hot strong coffee

Method:

1. *Pour the cold milk into a tall glass.*
2. *Attach the Drink Mixer to the Twist & Mix then set to the Drink Mixer Position.*
3. *Whisk on HIGH for 30 seconds or until soft peaks form.*
4. *Pour sweetened condensed milk into a coffee cup.*
5. *Pour hot coffee over the condensed milk into the cup.*
6. *Spoon frothed milk over coffee and serve immediately.*

OLD FASHIONED
WHIPPED CREAM

Makes 3 cups

Ingredients:

2 cups heavy cream, cold
1/4 cup granulated sugar
1/2 teaspoon vanilla extract

Method:

1. Place all ingredients into a narrow mixing bowl.
2. Attach the Wire Whisk to the Twist & Mix then set to the Whisk Position.
3. Whisk on HIGH for 2-3 minutes or until thick and soft peaks form.
4. Serve as desired. Briefly mix again if whipped cream sits for more than 30 minutes as the bottom will get watery and the foam will become dry.

TIP

For chocolate whipped cream add 2 tablespoons cocoa powder. For raspberry whipped cream add 1/4 cup Raspberry Sauce from page 82. For Coffee whipped cream add 1 tablespoon espresso powder.

BUTTERMILK
PIE

Makes 8 servings

Ingredients:

2/3 cup light brown sugar, packed

1/2 cup unsalted butter, melted

1 teaspoon vanilla extract

2 tablespoons apple cider vinegar

1/4 cup buttermilk

1/2 cup heavy whipping cream

8 large egg yolks

1 store-bought pie crust, unbaked

Powdered sugar, for dusting

Method:

1. *Preheat oven to 325°F.*
2. *Place all ingredients, except pie crust and powdered sugar, into a mixing bowl.*
3. *Attach the Wire Whisk to the Twist & Mix then set to the Whisk Position.*
4. *Whisk on LOW for 45 seconds or until smooth.*
5. *Place the pie crust into a pie pan.*
6. *Pour mixture into the pie crust then bake for 15 minutes.*
7. *After 15 minutes of baking, lower oven temperature to 300°F and bake for an additional 40 minutes or until set.*
8. *Remove and let cool for 1 hour.*
9. *Dust with powdered sugar and serve at room temperature.*

STRABERRY FRUIT
DIP

Makes 2-3 cups

Ingredients:

1 container (8 ounces) strawberry yogurt

1 container (8 ounces) sour cream

2 cups marshmallow crème

Assorted dippers, for serving

Method:

1. *Pour yogurt, sour cream and marshmallow crème into a mixing bowl.*
2. *Attach the Beater to the Twist & Mix then set to the Hand Mixer Position.*
3. *Mix on LOW then increase speed to HIGH and mix for 1-2 minutes or until smooth.*
4. *Serve with desired dippers.*

TIP

Change the flavor of the yogurt to make different tasting fruit dips.

HOMEMADE BUTTERCREAM
FROSTING

Makes about 5 cups

Ingredients:

1 cup unsalted butter, softened
2 teaspoons vanilla extract
Pinch of kosher salt
3 tablespoons heavy cream + more if needed
6 cups powdered sugar, sifted

Method:

1. Place the butter into a large mixing bowl.
2. Attach the Beater to the Twist & Mix then set to the Hand Mixer Position.
3. Beat on HIGH for 4-5 minutes or until smooth and no lumps remain then add remaining ingredients.
4. Mix on LOW until most of the powdered sugar is absorbed then increase speed to HIGH and mix for 2-3 minutes, scraping down the sides of the bowl occasionally.
5. If frosting is too thick, add some more cream, 1 teaspoon at a time, until desired consistency is achieved.
6. Use as desired.

TIP

For chocolate buttercream, add 2/3 cup sifted cocoa along with the powdered sugar and increase the cream to 1/2 cup.

CAKE BATTER
MILKSHAKE

Makes 1 serving

Ingredients:

4 big scoops vanilla ice cream

3 tablespoons boxed white cake mix, dry

1/8 teaspoon almond extract

1/2 cup whole milk

1 tablespoon confetti sprinkles + more for topping

Method:

1. *Place all ingredients into a tall drinking glass.*
2. *Attach the Drink Mixer to the Twist & Mix then set to the Drink Mixer Position.*
3. *Mix on LOW for a few seconds then increase speed to HIGH until smooth.*
4. *Top with additional confetti sprinkles, garnish as desired and serve immediately.*

COOKIES & MILK
SHOT GLASSES

Makes about 12 cookies

Ingredients:

1 cup unsalted butter, melted

2 cups all purpose flour

1 teaspoon baking soda

1 teaspoon kosher salt

1 cup granulated sugar

1/2 cup light brown sugar, packed

2 teaspoons vanilla extract

2 large eggs

2 cups semi-sweet chocolate chips + more for lining

Milk, for serving

Method:

1. *Preheat oven to 325° F and thoroughly apply nonstick cooking spray to a silicone shot glass mold pan.*

2. *Place all ingredients, except chocolate chips and milk, into a large mixing bowl.*

3. *Attach the Beater to the Twist & Mix then set to the Hand Mixer Position.*

4. *Mix on LOW for about 1 minute or until well blended.*

5. *Add the chocolate chips then mix just until uniform.*

6. *Using your fingers, fill the shot glass mold 2/3 full with dough.*

7. *Bake shot glasses for 30-35 minutes or until dark browned and firm.*

8. *Freeze cookies in mold until hard then peel out of mold.*

9. *Melt 1/4 cup additional chocolate chips in the microwave.*

10. *Using your finger or small spoon, coat the inside of each frozen cookie shot glass with chocolate then refreeze until ready to serve.*

11. *Remove from freezer a few minutes before serving then fill with milk.*

TIP

You can find the silicone shot glass mold pan in the cake decorating section of your retailer or online.

BANANA BREAD

Makes 1 loaf

Ingredients:

1/2 cup (1 stick) unsalted butter, softened

1 cup granulated sugar

4 large overripe bananas, sliced

2 large eggs

1 teaspoon vanilla extract

3 tablespoons sour cream

1/2 cup toasted walnuts, chopped

2 cups unbleached all purpose flour

1 teaspoon baking soda

1/2 teaspoon baking powder

1/2 teaspoon kosher salt

Method:

1. *Preheat oven to 350°F.*
2. *Lightly apply nonstick cooking spray to a loaf pan.*
3. *Place butter and sugar into a mixing bowl.*
4. *Attach the Beater to the Twist & Mix then set to the Hand Mixer Position.*
5. *Beat on LOW for 30 seconds, then increase speed to HIGH and beat for 1-2 minutes or until creamy.*
6. *Add the bananas, eggs, vanilla and sour cream then beat until combined and bananas are chopped.*
7. *Add remaining ingredients and beat for an additional 1-2 minutes or until combined.*
8. *Pour batter into prepared pan.*
9. *Bake for 50-60 minutes; to test for doneness insert a wooden pick off-center, it should come out with just a few moist crumbs clinging to it. If it has a streak of shiny batter on it, bake for an additional 5-10 minutes then test again.*
10. *Remove then let sit for 20-30 minutes before removing from pan.*
11. *Serve warm with butter.*

TIP

The best banana bread is made with bananas that are 5-7 days old. The bananas should be very soft and covered with spots for best flavor.

DUTCH BABY
PANCAKE

Makes 2-4 servings

Ingredients:

3/4 cup all purpose flour

3/4 cup whole milk

3 eggs

1/2 teaspoon kosher salt

3 tablespoons butter

3 cups mixed fresh berries

Maple syrup

Powdered sugar

Method:

1. *Place flour, milk, eggs and salt into a mixing bowl.*
2. *Attach the Wire Whisk to the Twist & Mix then set to the Whisk Position.*
3. *Whisk on HIGH for 1-2 minutes or until smooth; set aside.*
4. *Preheat oven to 450°F.*
5. *Position the oven rack in the upper 1/3 of the oven.*
6. *Place a 10-inch omelet pan with sloped sides on the oven rack and let preheat for 10 minutes.*
7. *Using pot holders, carefully pull out the oven rack halfway, add the butter to the omelet pan then close the oven door and let the butter melt for 3 minutes.*
8. *Carefully pull out the oven rack again and pour the batter into the center of the omelet pan without splashing the batter.*
9. *Bake for 20-25 minutes or until puffed into a bowl shape and deep brown in color.*
10. *Remove pan from oven using pot holders and set on a heat-proof surface.*
11. *Pour berries into the center then top as desired with syrup and powdered sugar before serving.*

BANANA MILKSHAKE

Makes 1 serving

Ingredients:

4 big scoops vanilla ice cream
1/4 teaspoon banana extract (optional)
1 ripe banana
1/2 cup whole milk
Old Fashioned Whipped Cream, for topping (see page 24)
Maraschino cherry, for topping

Method:

1. *Place all ingredients, except whipped cream and cherry, into a tall drinking glass.*
2. *Attach the Drink Mixer to the Twist & Mix then set to the Drink Mixer Position.*
3. *Mix on LOW for a few seconds then increase speed to HIGH until smooth.*
4. *Garnish with whipped cream and maraschino cherry before serving.*

CARROT ZUCCHINI
BREAD

Makes 1 loaf

Ingredients:

2 cups zucchini, shredded

2/3 cup carrot, shredded

1/2 cup vegetable oil

2 large eggs

1/4 cup sour cream

1 tablespoon lemon juice

2 cups unbleached all purpose flour

1 teaspoon baking soda

1 teaspoon baking powder

1/4 teaspoon ground cinnamon

1 1/4 teaspoons kosher salt

1/2 cup pecan pieces, toasted

Method:

1. *Preheat oven to 350°F.*
2. *Lightly apply nonstick cooking spray to a loaf pan.*
3. *Place all ingredients into a mixing bowl.*
4. *Attach the Beater to the Twist & Mix then set to the Hand Mixer Position.*
5. *Beat on LOW for 30 seconds then increase speed to HIGH and mix for 2-3 minutes or until combined.*
6. *Pour batter into the prepared loaf pan.*
7. *Bake for 50-60 minutes; to test for doneness insert a wooden pick off-center, it should come out with just a few moist crumbs clinging to it. If it has a streak of shiny batter on it, bake for an additional 5-10 minutes then test again.*
8. *Let cool for 20 minutes before removing from loaf pan.*
9. *Garnish as desired and serve warm.*

If your zucchini is wet after grating, pat dry with paper towels before adding to the recipe. Young zucchini contain more moisture than old and excess moisture will make a gummy layer at the bottom of the loaf.

BREAKFAST EGG
CUPS

Makes 6 cups

Ingredients:

Unsalted butter, softened, for spreading

6 sandwich bread slices

6 large eggs

6 Canadian bacon slices, diced

1/2 cup Swiss or Cheddar cheese, grated

1 green onion, thinly sliced

Kosher salt and fresh pepper to taste

Method:

1. *Preheat oven to 350°F.*
2. *Apply nonstick cooking spray to a large size 6-spot muffin tin.*
3. *Butter one side of each bread slice then press a slice, butter-side down, into each muffin tin well.*
4. *Place eggs into a mixing bowl.*
5. *Attach the Beater to the Twist & Mix then set to the Hand Mixer Position.*
6. *Beat eggs on LOW for 15-20 seconds.*
7. *Add remaining ingredients to the bowl then beat on LOW for an additional 5 seconds just to combine.*
8. *Divide the egg mixture evenly then pour over the bread into each muffin tin well.*
9. *Bake for 20-30 minutes or until eggs are puffed and edges of bread are turning brown.*
10. *Remove, garnish as desired and serve hot.*

WOLF'S FAVORITE
CHEESECAKE

Makes 1 cake

Ingredients:

1 pound cream cheese, softened

2 cups granulated sugar

3 large eggs

1 store-bought chocolate cookie pie crust

Method:

1. *Preheat oven to 350°F.*
2. *Place the cream cheese and sugar into a mixing bowl.*
3. *Attach the Beater to the Twist & Mix then set to the Hand Mixer Position.*
4. *Beat on LOW for 1 minute or until smooth.*
5. *Scrape down the sides of the bowl using a spatula then beat for an additional 1 minute.*
6. *Add the eggs, beat for 1 minute then scrape down the bowl again and beat for an additional 30 seconds just to incorporate the eggs.*
7. *Pour batter into the pie crust (pie crust does not need to be baked first).*
8. *Bake for 30-40 minutes or until puffed and golden brown.*
9. *Remove, garnish as desired then serve hot, warm or cold.*

TIP

Store-bought chocolate cookie crusts are found in the baking section of your grocery store next to the gelatin. There is no need to use a separate baking pan as these come prebaked and pressed into a disposable aluminum pan.

FRIED PEACH
FRITTERS

Makes 4 servings

Ingredients:

Canola oil, for frying

2 large eggs

1 1/2 cups all purpose flour

1/4 teaspoon baking powder

1/4 teaspoon kosher salt

2 tablespoons unsalted butter

2 tablespoons brown sugar

1 teaspoon fresh lemon juice

1 teaspoon vanilla extract

3/4 cup club soda, ice cold

4 very ripe peaches, sliced

Powdered sugar, for serving

Peach ice cream (optional)

Method:

1. *In a large, heavy Dutch oven, preheat 2-inches of oil to 350°F using a thermometer.*
2. *Place eggs in a mixing bowl.*
3. *Attach the Beater to the Twist & Mix then set to the Hand Mixer Position.*
4. *Beat eggs on HIGH for 2 minutes or until very light in color then reduce speed to LOW and add the flour, baking powder, salt, butter, brown sugar, lemon juice and vanilla. Mix for 1-2 minutes to combine then mix in the club soda until just incorporated.*
5. *Dip a few peach slices into the batter, turn to coat evenly then let excess batter drip off.*
6. *Using tongs, place peach slices into the Dutch oven and fry for 2 minutes on each side or until golden brown.*
7. *Remove, drain on absorbent paper and repeat with remaining peaches.*
8. *Sprinkle with powdered sugar while still hot.*
9. *Garnish as desired and serve warm with peach ice cream.*

OLD FASHIONED STRAWBERRY
MILKSHAKE

Makes 1 serving

Ingredients:

4 large strawberries, diced

1 tablespoon granulated sugar

1/2 cup whole milk

4 big scoops strawberry ice cream

Method:

1. *Place strawberries and sugar into a tall drinking glass.*
2. *Attach the Drink Mixer to the Twist & Mix then set to the Drink Mixer Position.*
3. *Mix on LOW for 10 seconds to break up the strawberries.*
4. *Add remaining ingredients to the glass.*
5. *Mix on LOW then increase speed to HIGH and mix until smooth.*
6. *Garnish as desired and serve immediately.*

7 MINUTE
FROSTING

Makes 5 cups

Ingredients:

2 large egg whites
2 tablespoons light corn syrup
1 1/2 cups granulated sugar
5 tablespoons water
1/4 teaspoon cream of tartar
1/8 teaspoon kosher salt
1 teaspoon pure vanilla extract
1/8 teaspoon butter-vanilla extract (see source page 108)

Method:

1. *Fashion a double boiler by setting a metal or heat-proof glass bowl over a saucepan so that it nests comfortably. Bring 2 inches of water to a simmer over medium heat (the bottom of the bowl should not touch the water).*

2. *Combine all ingredients, except vanilla and butter-vanilla extracts, in the double boiler.*

3. *Attach the Beater to the Twist & Mix then set to the Hand Mixer Position.*

4. *Beat on LOW for a few seconds or until moistened then increase speed to HIGH and beat for 6-7 minutes or until very billowy and peaks form.*

5. *Add remaining ingredients and mix just to incorporate.*

6. *Use the frosting right away, as it will form a crust after about 15 minutes.*

7. *This frosting is typically piled on cakes quite thickly then swirled into waves and peaks using the back of a spoon or a spatula.*

TIP

This frosting is great on the Vanilla Cupcakes on page 22.

CORN & BACON
CHEESE DIP

Makes 3 cups

Ingredients:

2 packages (8 ounces each) cream cheese, softened

1 bunch green onions, thinly sliced

1/2 cup grape tomatoes, quartered

1/2 cup goat cheese or Parmesan cheese, crumbled

Kosher salt and fresh pepper to taste

Hot sauce, to taste

1/4 cup mayonnaise

1/3 cup cooked bacon, crumbled

1 can (15 ounces) corn, drained

Assorted dippers

Method:

1. *Preheat oven to 375°F and apply nonstick cooking spray to an 8x8-inch baking dish.*
2. *Place all ingredients, except dippers, into a large mixing bowl.*
3. *Attach the Beater to the Twist & Mix then set to the Hand Mixer Position.*
4. *Mix on LOW for a few seconds then increase speed to HIGH and mix for 2-3 minutes or until well mixed.*
5. *Scrape mixture into prepared baking dish and smooth the top.*
6. *Bake for 25-30 minutes or until browned and bubbly.*
7. *Serve hot or warm with assorted dippers of your choice.*

MASHED
SWEET POTATOES

Makes 6 servings

Ingredients:

4 pounds sweet potatoes, peeled and chunked

Kosher salt to taste

1/3 cup unsalted butter

Pinch of ground cinnamon (optional)

1-2 tablespoons light brown sugar, packed (optional)

Method:

1. *Place potatoes and some salt into a large pot then add cold water until potatoes are covered by 1-inch of water.*
2. *Bring to a boil over high heat then reduce heat to a simmer.*
3. *Let potatoes simmer for 15 minutes or until tender.*
4. *Drain potatoes thoroughly, reserving 1/2 cup of the water.*
5. *Season with additional salt, then add the butter as well as cinnamon and brown sugar if desired.*
6. *Attach the Beater to the Twist & Mix then set to the Hand Mixer Position.*
7. *Mix on LOW then increase speed to HIGH and mix until texture is fairly smooth, adding some of the reserved water if potatoes are too thick.*
8. *Garnish as desired and serve hot.*

BEST BAKED
MEATBALLS

Makes about 15 meatballs

Ingredients:

1 pound lean ground beef

1 large egg

2 white bread slices, torn into bits

1/4 cup half & half or whole milk

1 tablespoon beef-flavored bouillon base

2 garlic cloves, minced

2 tablespoons yellow mustard

1 small yellow onion, minced

1 teaspoon dried sage

2 teaspoons kosher salt and fresh pepper or to taste

Method:

1. *Preheat oven to 375°F.*
2. *Place all ingredients into a mixing bowl.*
3. *Attach the Beater to the Twist & Mix then set to the Hand Mixer Position.*
4. *Mix for 1 minute to combine; do not over mix.*
5. *Using wet hands, roll mixture into 15 balls then place onto a greased sheet pan.*
6. *Bake for 25-30 minutes or until internal temperature reads 165°F on a thermometer.*
7. *Remove, garnish as desired and serve.*

CRISPY BATTERED
VEGETABLES

Makes 4-6 servings

Ingredients:

2 cups complete buttermilk pancake mix

2 cups cold water

Kosher salt and fresh pepper to taste

1/2 teaspoon garlic powder

Bottled hot sauce, to taste

Oil, such as Canola, for frying

2 green onions, cut into 2-inch pieces

1 medium yellow onion, sliced

1 cup snow peas

1 cup small broccoli florets

1 cup green beans, halved

2 carrots, sliced

Bottled sweet chili sauce, for serving

Method:

1. *Place the pancake mix, water, salt, pepper, garlic powder and hot sauce into a narrow mixing bowl.*
2. *Attach the Wire Whisk to the Twist & Mix then set to the Whisk Position.*
3. *Whisk on LOW for 30 seconds or until batter is fairly smooth with a few lumps.*
4. *In a large, heavy Dutch oven, heat 2-inches of oil to 350°F using a thermometer.*
5. *Using tongs, dip a few vegetables into the batter then allow excess batter to drip off before adding to the oil.*
6. *Fry for 2 minutes on each side or until browned and crispy.*
7. *Remove and drain on absorbent paper then salt immediately.*
8. *Repeat with remaining vegetables.*
9. *Serve immediately with sweet chili sauce for dipping.*

EASY SAUSAGE
PASTA

Makes 6-8 servings

Ingredients:

8 ounces cream cheese, softened

1 cup Parmesan cheese, grated

2 large eggs

Kosher salt and fresh pepper to taste

1 cup whole milk

3 cups pasta sauce

2 cups mozzarella cheese, grated

1 pound Italian sausage, cooked and sliced

1 package (12 ounces) frozen broccoli florets

1 pound dry pasta, cooked

Method:

1. Preheat oven to 350°F then apply nonstick cooking spray to a 9x13-inch baking dish.
2. Place cream cheese, Parmesan, eggs, salt and pepper into a large mixing bowl.
3. Attach the Beater to the Twist & Mix then set to the Hand Mixer Position.
4. Mix on LOW for a few seconds then increase speed to HIGH and mix for 1 minute or until blended.
5. Add the milk, pasta sauce and mozzarella then mix on LOW until blended.
6. Place the sausage, broccoli and pasta into the prepared baking dish.
7. Pour the cream cheese mixture over the baking dish contents then spread evenly using a spatula.
8. Bake for 40-50 minutes or until brown and bubbly.
9. Remove, garnish as desired and serve hot.

CREAMY PESTO
CHICKEN BAKE

Makes 6 servings

Ingredients:

1 package (8 ounces) cream cheese, softened

1 cup Parmesan cheese, grated

3 large eggs

Kosher salt and fresh pepper to taste

1/2 cup jarred pesto

1 1/2 cups whole milk

1 cup sun-dried tomatoes, sliced

2 cups leftover rotisserie chicken, chopped

2 cups mozzarella cheese, grated

1 package (10 ounces) frozen peas

1 pound dry pasta, cooked

Method:

1. *Preheat oven to 350°F and apply nonstick cooking spray to a 9x13-inch baking dish.*

2. *Place the cream cheese, Parmesan, eggs, salt and pepper into a large mixing bowl.*

3. *Attach the Beater to the Twist & Mix then set to the Hand Mixer Position.*

4. *Mix on LOW for a few seconds then increase speed to HIGH and mix for 1 minute or until blended.*

5. *Add the pesto, milk, sun-dried tomatoes, chicken and mozzarella then mix on LOW until blended.*

6. *Place the peas and pasta into the prepared baking dish.*

7. *Pour the cream cheese mixture over the baking dish contents and spread evenly using a spatula.*

8. *Bake for 40-50 minutes or until brown and bubbly.*

9. *Remove, garnish as desired and serve hot.*

EASY FLAN

Makes 1 flan

Ingredients:

For the Microwave Caramel:

4 tablespoons granulated sugar

2 teaspoons water

For the Flan:

1 cup evaporated milk

1 cup condensed milk

3 large eggs

6 large egg yolks

1 teaspoon vanilla extract

Method:

1. *To make the microwave caramel, place sugar and water into a microwave-safe bowl.*
2. *Microwave on high for 1-2 minutes or until bubbly and mixture turns amber in color.*
3. *Line a 6-inch cake pan with the microwave caramel then set aside.*
4. *Preheat oven to 300°F.*
5. *Place all flan ingredients into a mixing bowl.*
6. *Attach the Wire Whisk to the Twist & Mix then set to the Whisk Position.*
7. *Whisk on LOW for 1 minute to incorporate.*
8. *Pour mixture into pan then cover with aluminum foil (you may have extra if your pan is short).*
9. *Create a water bath by placing the 6-inch cake pan into an 8-inch (or larger) pan. Fill larger pan with hot water until half way up the sides of the 6-inch cake pan.*
10. *Bake for 50-60 minutes or until a small knife inserted off-center comes out clean.*
11. *Refrigerate flan for a minimum of 2 hours or up to 3 days.*
12. *Garnish as desired and serve cold.*

TIP

You can flavor this recipe in many ways. For chocolate flan, add 1/3 cup of cocoa powder. For lemon flan, add the zest of 2 lemons + 1 tablespoon of lemon juice. For ginger flan, add 2 teaspoons of ground ginger powder. For maple flan, add 2 tablespoons maple syrup + 1/2 teaspoon maple extract.

CHOCOLATE CRINKLE COOKIES

Makes about 24 cookies

Ingredients:

1/4 cup vegetable oil

1 large egg

1 large egg yolk

1 tablespoon light corn syrup

1/2 cup semi-sweet chocolate chips, melted, slightly cooled

1 1/4 cups granulated sugar

1 teaspoon baking powder

1/4 teaspoon kosher salt

1 teaspoon vanilla extract

3/4 cup all purpose flour

Granulated sugar, for rolling

Powdered sugar, for rolling

Method:

1. *Place all ingredients, except sugars for rolling, into a mixing bowl.*
2. *Attach the Beater to the Twist & Mix then set to the Hand Mixer Position.*
3. *Beat on LOW for 15 seconds then increase speed to HIGH and beat for 45 seconds or until smooth.*
4. *Covering mixing bowl and chill dough for 1-2 hours.*
5. *Preheat oven to 350°F and line a sheet pan with parchment paper.*
6. *Scoop up dough using a small ice cream scoop.*
7. *Roll the dough scoops between your hands to form balls.*
8. *Roll each ball in sugar then powdered sugar until thoroughly coated.*
9. *Place the dough balls on the sheet pan about 3-inches apart.*
10. *Bake for 15 minutes or until puffed and cracked.*
11. *Remove and let cool for 5-10 minutes.*
12. *Serve warm.*

CHOCOLATE
CUPCAKES

Makes about 12 cupcakes

Ingredients:

1 cup unsalted butter, softened

3 cups light brown sugar, packed

4 large eggs

1 tablespoon vanilla extract

1 1/2 cups sour cream

1 1/3 cups water

2/3 cup quality cocoa powder

2 teaspoons baking soda

1/2 teaspoon kosher salt

2 cups cake flour

Method:

1. *Prepare a cupcake pan with papers and set aside.*
2. *Place butter and sugar into a mixing bowl.*
3. *Attach the Beater to the Twist & Mix then set to the Hand Mixer Position.*
4. *Beat on LOW for 1 minute then increase speed to HIGH and beat for 2 minutes or until fluffy.*
5. *While beating, add the eggs as well as the vanilla and beat until smooth.*
6. *Add the sour cream and water then beat until smooth.*
7. *Sift the cocoa powder, baking soda, salt and flour at the same time then add to the bowl and beat until smooth.*
8. *Using an ice cream scoop, place batter into the cupcake papers until each is 3/4 full.*
9. *Preheat oven to 350°F.*
10. *Bake for 20 minutes or until puffed and set.*
11. *Remove and let cool completely.*
12. *Frost as desired before serving.*

TIP

Ice these cupcakes with the
Homemade Buttercream
Frosting on page 27 or the
7 Minute Frosting on page 40.

APPLE CIDER CAKE
WITH APPLE ICING

Makes 1 stacked cake

Ingredients:

For the Cake:

1 1/2 cups unbleached all purpose flour

2 teaspoons baking powder

1/2 teaspoon kosher salt

1/4 teaspoon ground cinnamon

2/3 cup apple cider

2 teaspoons fresh lemon juice

1/2 cup unsalted butter

1 cup granulated sugar

3 large eggs

For the Apple Icing:

3/4 cup granulated sugar

3 tablespoons corn starch

1/8 teaspoon kosher salt

3/4 cup apple cider

1 1/4 cups unsalted butter

Method:

1. Preheat oven to 350°F.
2. Grease two 8-inch round cake pans; set aside.
3. In a bowl, sift flour, baking powder, salt and cinnamon; set aside.
4. In a measuring cup, combine the apple cider and lemon juice; set aside.
5. Place butter and sugar into a large mixing bowl.
6. Attach the Beater to the Twist & Mix then set to the Hand Mixer Position.
7. Beat the butter-sugar mixture on LOW for 60 seconds.
8. While beating, add the eggs, one at a time, to the butter mixture (the mixture will look curdled). Add the flour mixture and cider mixture and continue to beat until smooth.
9. Divide the mixture between the two greased cake pans (the mixture will be low in the pan).
10. Bake for 25-30 minutes; to test for doneness insert a wooden pick off-center, it should come out with just a few moist crumbs clinging to it.
11. Remove and let cool then refrigerate for a minimum of 4 hours or until cold.
12. To make the icing, combine the sugar, corn starch and salt in a 2-quart heavy saucepan.
13. Attach the Wire Whisk to the Twist & Mix then set to the Hand Mixer Position.
14. Whisk in the apple cider on LOW and bring to a boil over medium heat (whisk constantly until mixture becomes very thick).
15. Transfer the mixture to a mixing bowl then place the mixing bowl into a larger bowl holding ice cold water and stir occasionally until cool (about 15 minutes).
16. Attach the Beater to the Twist & Mix then set to the Hand Mixer Position.
17. Place the butter into a separate bowl then beat on HIGH until light and fluffy.
18. Pour cider mixture into the butter and mix on HIGH until light and smooth.
19. Ice each cake layer with the apple icing then stack if desired and serve.

TIP

Unfiltered apple cider has the strongest flavor and will make the best tasting cake. If you can't find it, add 1/2 teaspoon of apple extract.

COCONUT COFFEE CREAMER

Makes 2 cups

Ingredients:

2 cans (13.5 ounces each) regular coconut milk (not light), chilled for a minimum of 24 hours
1/4 cup granulated sugar or a sugar substitute such as stevia
1 teaspoon vanilla extract
Small pinch of kosher salt

Method:

1. *Open both cans of coconut milk.*
2. *Scoop off the thicker part of one can and transfer to a mixing bowl (reserve the milky part of this can for another use).*
3. *Add all of the second can into the mixing bowl then add remaining ingredients.*
4. *Attach the Wire Whisk to the Twist & Mix then set to the Whisk Position.*
5. *Whisk on HIGH for 1 minute or until frothy.*
6. *Use as desired or store in an airtight container in the refrigerator for up to 1 week.*

TIP

Because this creamer requires the coconut milk to be chilled for a long time, I always keep extra unopened cans of coconut milk in my fridge so I can make this creamer whenever I want.

COCONUT MILK
WHIPPED CREAM

Makes 1 cup

Ingredients:

2 cans (13.5 ounces each) regular coconut milk (not light), chilled for a minimum of 24 hours

1/2 teaspoon vanilla extract

1/3 cup powdered sugar

Method:

1. Refrigerate coconut milk for a minimum of 24 hours as it must be very cold to achieve the desired outcome.

2. Place a narrow mixing bowl and the Twist & Mix's Wire Whisk attachment in the freezer for 10 minutes or until cold.

3. Open the cold cans of coconut milk and scoop out the more solid part of each can (reserve the milky part for another use) into the chilled mixing bowl then add remaining ingredients.

4. Attach the Wire Whisk to the Twist & Mix then set to the Whisk Position.

5. Whisk on HIGH for 2-3 minutes or until thick.

6. Cover bowl and refrigerate for a minimum of 1 hour or until solid enough to scoop.

7. Use as desired.

HOMEMADE MARSHMALLOWS

Makes about 60 marshmallows

Ingredients:

2 cups corn starch + more if desired, for dusting

2 tablespoons unflavored gelatin

3 tablespoons + 2/3 cup cold water

1 2/3 cups granulated sugar

1 1/2 cups light corn syrup

2/3 cup water

3 large egg whites

2 teaspoons vanilla extract

TIP

Read through this recipe before starting. You will see that corn starch is used to prevent sticking. You can use it on the sheet pan, the cutting board, the knife and your hands.

Method:

1. Sift some corn starch in an even layer over a 1/4 sheet pan; set aside.
2. Attach the Wire Whisk to the Twist & Mix then set to the Whisk Position.
3. Place the gelatin and 3 tablespoons water into a mixing bowl.
4. Immediately whisk on LOW for 10 seconds to incorporate then set aside and let rest for 5 minutes.
5. In a 4-quart saucepan over medium-high heat, combine sugar, corn syrup and remaining 2/3 cup cold water; heat for a few minutes until temperature reaches 242°F on a thermometer.
6. Immediately pour the hot syrup over the gelatin in the mixing bowl and whisk on HIGH for 5 minutes.
7. Add remaining ingredients, except remaining corn starch, and mix on HIGH until the mixture quadruples in volume.
8. Scrape the marshmallow mixture onto the prepared 1/4 sheet pan.
9. Sift remaining corn starch over the top and let cool for 2 hours at room temperature.
10. Using your fingers, pry the sheet of marshmallow from the pan then place it on a cutting board.
11. Using a knife, trim the edges and cut into even squares.
12. Roll marshmallows in additional corn starch, shake off the excess and serve.

CHOCOLATE
BABY CAKES

Makes about 10 baby cakes

Ingredients:

4 ounces cream cheese, softened

3/4 cup (1 1/2 sticks) unsalted butter, softened

1 1/2 cups granulated sugar

3 large eggs

1 teaspoon pure vanilla extract (see source page 108)

1/2 teaspoon kosher salt

1 1/4 cups unbleached all purpose flour

1/4 cup cocoa powder

Powdered sugar, for serving

Method:

1. *Preheat oven to 325°F.*
2. *Place cream cheese, butter and sugar into a mixing bowl.*
3. *Attach the Beater to the Twist & Mix then set to the Hand Mixer Position.*
4. *Beat on LOW for 1 minute then increase speed to HIGH and beat for 2-3 minutes or until fluffy.*
5. *Add eggs to the bowl and beat until incorporated.*
6. *Scrape down sides of the bowl using a spatula then add remaining ingredients, except powdered sugar, and beat until just smooth.*
7. *Scrape batter into greased baby cake or mini loaf pans until 3/4 full.*
8. *Bake for 25 minutes; to test for doneness insert a wooden pick off-center, it should come out with just a few moist crumbs clinging to it.*
9. *Let cool for 20 minutes before removing from the pans.*
10. *Dust with powdered sugar, garnish as desired and serve.*

GLUTEN-FREE PEANUT BUTTER COOKIES

Makes about 18 cookies

Ingredients:

2 cups smooth peanut butter

2 cups granulated sugar + more for topping

1/4 teaspoon kosher salt

1 teaspoon baking soda

2 large eggs

2 tablespoons corn starch

2 teaspoons vanilla extract

Method:

1. Preheat oven to 325°F.
2. Place all ingredients into a mixing bowl.
3. Attach the Beater to the Twist & Mix then set to the Hand Mixer Position.
4. Beat on LOW for 1-2 minutes or until combined.
5. Divide the dough and form it into 18 balls.
6. Place the balls onto parchment-lined cookie sheets.
7. Pat down the top of each ball with the palm of your hand.
8. Sprinkle the tops with additional sugar.
9. Press the tines of a fork twice into each dough ball to form a crisscross pattern.
10. Bake for 12-18 minutes or until slightly puffed and brown.
11. Remove, garnish as desired and serve warm.

CREAM PUFFS

Makes 12 servings

Ingredients:

1 cup water
1/4 cup unsalted butter
1 teaspoon kosher salt
1 teaspoon granulated sugar
1 cup bread flour
4 large eggs
2 large egg whites, divided

TIP

Fill cream puffs with the Old Fashioned Whipped Cream on page 24, Lemon Curd on page 12 or make it savory and fill with chicken salad.

RECIPES

60

Method:

1. *Line two 1/4 sheet pans with aluminum foil; set aside.*
2. *In a large saucepan, combine the water, butter, salt and sugar; bring to a boil.*
3. *Using a wooden spoon, stir in all of the flour at once then stir vigorously for 1 minute while still on the stove until a solid ball of dough forms.*
4. *Attach the Beater to the Twist & Mix then set to the Hand Mixer Position.*
5. *Add the 4 eggs and 1 egg white.*
6. *Beat on LOW for 1 minute then increase speed to HIGH and beat for 2 minutes until smooth and uniform in color; scrape down the sides of the saucepan using the spoon.*
7. *Test the consistency by pinching a small amount of dough between your thumb and index finger then pull your fingers apart. The dough should stretch out into a 2-inch strand. If it breaks before 2-inches, there is not enough egg so add remaining egg white.*
8. *Scoop cream puff dough into 2-inch balls onto 1/4 sheet pans (6 balls per pan).*
9. *Sprinkle tops with droplets of water and pat down any points.*
10. *Preheat oven to 425°F.*
11. *Bake for 20 minutes then reduce oven temperature to 350°F and continue to bake for an additional 30 minutes or until puffs have tripled in size and are a deep brown color.*
12. *Remove and let cool before serving.*

SHREDDED PORK
CARNITAS

Makes 4-6 servings

Ingredients:

4 pounds boneless pork shoulder, cut into chunks

3 tablespoons pork or chicken-flavored bouillon base

Kosher salt and fresh pepper to taste

4 garlic cloves, left whole

1 large yellow onion, chopped

3 tablespoons fresh lime juice

1/2 teaspoon ground cumin

1/2 teaspoon oregano

2 cups water

Method:

1. *Preheat oven to 350°F.*
2. *Place all ingredients into a large Dutch oven; stir then cover tightly.*
3. *Bake for 3 hours or until pork is very tender.*
4. *Remove and let cool for 15 minutes then drain off and reserve the juices from the Dutch oven and remove visible large pieces of fat from the pork.*
5. *Attach the Beater to the Twist & Mix then set to the Hand Mixer Position.*
6. *Use your Twist & Mix on LOW to break up and shred the tender pork meat.*
7. *When thoroughly shredded, return the reserved juices to the meat.*
8. *Garnish as desired and serve.*

TIP
This recipe can also be made using a pressure cooker in 30 minutes.

EGG SALAD

Makes 2 cups

Ingredients:

6 large hard boiled eggs

2 tablespoons store-bought sweet pickle relish

1/3 cup Homemade Mayonnaise (see page 100)

1 tablespoon yellow mustard

3 tablespoons unsalted butter, softened

Kosher salt and fresh pepper to taste

Sandwich fixings of your choice, for serving

Method:

1. *Place all ingredients, except sandwich fixings, into a mixing bowl.*
2. *Attach the Beater to the Twist & Mix then set to the Hand Mixer Position.*
3. *Press the Beater into each hard boiled egg to break it up a bit.*
4. *Mix on LOW for a few seconds then increase speed to HIGH until chunky.*
5. *Garnish as desired and serve on sandwiches.*

MUSHROOM LETTUCE WRAPS
WITH PEANUT SAUCE

Makes 8 servings

Ingredients:

2 tablespoons vegetable oil

1 package (8 ounces) white mushrooms, chopped

1 large yellow onion, chopped

4 garlic cloves, minced

2 coins fresh ginger, minced

1 can (4 ounces) diced water chestnuts, drained

2 tablespoons soy sauce

1 tablespoon dark sesame oil

1 bunch green onions, chopped

Iceberg lettuce leaves, for serving

Sriracha hot sauce, for serving

For the Peanut Sauce:

1 cup natural peanut butter

1/3 cup hot water

1/4 cup hoisin sauce

2 tablespoons soy sauce

2 tablespoons light brown sugar, packed

Method:

1. *Preheat the oil in a large skillet over medium-high heat.*
2. *When oil is hot, add the mushrooms, onions, garlic, ginger and water chestnuts; cook while stirring constantly for 5 minutes or until well browned.*
3. *Add the soy sauce, sesame oil and green onions then stir thoroughly and remove from heat.*
4. *Place all peanut sauce ingredients into a small bowl.*
5. *Attach the Wire Whisk to the Twist & Mix then set to the Whisk Position.*
6. *Whisk on LOW then increase speed to HIGH and whisk for 1 minute or until smooth and emulsified.*
7. *Wrap mushroom mixture in lettuce leaves and top with peanut sauce and sriracha.*

TIP

If you are allergic to peanuts, you can make this sauce with any other nut butter you are able to eat

PHILADELPHIA
CHICKEN BAKE

Makes 6-8 servings

Ingredients:

8 ounces cream cheese, softened

1 cup Parmesan cheese, grated

2 large eggs

Kosher salt and fresh pepper to taste

1 cup whole milk

3 cups pasta sauce

2 cups mozzarella cheese, grated

2 cups leftover rotisserie chicken, chopped

1 package (12 ounces) frozen broccoli florets

1 pound dry pasta, cooked

Method:

1. *Preheat oven to 350°F and apply nonstick cooking spray to a 9x13-inch baking dish.*
2. *Place cream cheese, Parmesan, eggs, salt and pepper into a large mixing bowl.*
3. *Attach the Beater to the Twist & Mix then set to the Hand Mixer Position.*
4. *Mix on LOW then increase speed to HIGH and mix for 1 minute or until blended.*
5. *While mixing on LOW, add the milk, pasta sauce and mozzarella until blended.*
6. *Place the chicken, broccoli and pasta into the baking dish.*
7. *Pour cream cheese mixture over the baking dish contents then spread evenly using a spatula.*
8. *Bake for 25-30 minutes or until brown and bubbly.*
9. *Remove, garnish as desired and serve hot.*

QUINOA KALE
VEGGIE BURGERS

Makes 8 servings

Ingredients:

3 tablespoons coconut or olive oil + more for cooking

4 kale leaves, chopped

4 garlic cloves, chopped

1 large yellow onion, chopped

1 package (8 ounces) white mushrooms, chopped

2 cups quinoa, cooked

1/2 cup diced tomato

2 tablespoons bottled soy sauce

1/2 cup black olives, chopped

Kosher salt and fresh pepper to taste

1 cup vital wheat gluten

Buns and desired toppings, for serving

Method:

1. *Preheat oven to 400°F and apply nonstick cooking spray to a large sheet pan.*
2. *Scatter all ingredients, except vital wheat gluten, buns and toppings, across the sheet pan.*
3. *Bake for 15 minutes, then stir and bake for an additional 15 minutes (this step is important as it removes excess moisture in the vegetables which allows for a better texture in the burger).*
4. *Transfer cooked mixture to a large mixing bowl then add the vital wheat gluten.*
5. *Attach the Beater to the Twist & Mix then set to the Hand Mixer Position.*
6. *Mix on LOW for 2 minutes or until mixture stiffens.*
7. *Shape mixture into 8 burgers patties, brushing both sides with additional oil.*
8. *Preheat a large skillet or grill to medium-high heat.*
9. *Cook patties on each side for 3-4 minutes or until crusty and well browned.*
10. *Serve with buns and toppings of your choice.*

TIP

Cooked burger patties freeze well for up to 3 months.

GLUTEN-FREE
PANCAKES

Makes 12 pancakes

Ingredients:

1/3 cup sour cream

1/2 teaspoon vanilla extract

1/2 teaspoon apple cider vinegar

2 cups buttermilk

3 large eggs

2 cups store-bought gluten-free baking mix

1 teaspoon kosher salt

2 tablespoons granulated sugar

1/2 teaspoon baking soda

1 teaspoon baking powder

Butter and syrup, for serving

Method:

1. *Preheat an electric griddle to 350°F or a pan over medium heat.*
2. *Place sour cream, vanilla, vinegar, buttermilk and eggs into a large mixing bowl.*
3. *Attach the Beater to the Twist & Mix then set to the Hand Mixer Position.*
4. *Mix on LOW for a few seconds then increase speed to HIGH for 30 seconds.*
5. *Add remaining ingredients, except butter and syrup, then mix on LOW to incorporate; do not over mix and allow some lumps to remain which will allow for fluffy pancakes.*
6. *Let batter rest for 5 minutes.*
7. *Ladle batter onto griddle/into pan and cook for about 2 minutes on each side.*
8. *Remove and repeat with remaining batter to make additional pancakes.*
9. *Garnish as desired and serve hot with butter and syrup.*

CHOCOLATE LAYER CAKE

Makes 1 cake

Ingredients:

1/2 cup unsalted butter, softened

1 1/2 cups light brown sugar, packed

2 large eggs

2 teaspoons vanilla extract

1/2 cup cocoa powder

2 teaspoons baking soda

1 1/2 cups cake flour

2/3 cup sour cream

1 teaspoon instant coffee granules

2/3 cup water

Homemade Buttercream Frosting (see page 27)

Method:

1. *Preheat oven to 350°F.*
2. *Butter and flour two 8-inch cake pans; set aside.*
3. *Place butter and brown sugar into a mixing bowl.*
4. *Attach the Beater to the Twist & Mix then set to the Hand Mixer Position.*
5. *Beat on LOW for 1 minute then increase speed to HIGH and beat for 2 minutes or until smooth.*
6. *Add eggs and vanilla extract then mix until combined.*
7. *Scrape down the bowl using a spatula then add remaining ingredients, except Homemade Buttercream Frosting, and mix until smooth.*
8. *Divide the batter between the two cake pans (the batter will be low in the pan).*
9. *Bake for 20-25 minutes; to test for doneness insert a wooden pick off-center, it should come out with just a few moist crumbs clinging to it.*
10. *Let cool for 10 minutes before unmolding one cake onto a serving platter. Top with a few spoonfuls of frosting and spread to the edge then stack and repeat with second layer.*

LOADED CANDY
COOKIE BARS

Makes about 14 bars

Ingredients:

For the Crust:

1 1/2 cups all purpose flour

1/4 cup powdered sugar

1/2 cup unsalted butter, melted

1 teaspoon vanilla extract

For the Filling:

4 eggs

1 cup light brown sugar, packed

2 tablespoons all purpose flour

1/2 teaspoon kosher salt

1/2 teaspoon vanilla extract

1/2 cup chocolate sandwich cookies, crushed

1/2 cup dark chocolate chips

1 cup mini marshmallows

1/2 cup colorful chocolate candy pieces

Method:

1. *Preheat oven to 350°F.*
2. *In a bowl, combine all crust ingredients; mix using a fork until a crumbly dough forms.*
3. *Press the dough into the bottom of a greased baking pan.*
4. *Bake for 15-20 minutes or until very light golden brown in color.*
5. *Place all filling ingredients, except chocolate candy pieces, into a large mixing bowl.*
6. *Attach the Beater to the Twist & Mix then set to the Hand Mixer Position.*
7. *Mix on LOW then increase speed to HIGH and mix for 30 seconds or until no egg remains visible.*
8. *Pour filling over the hot crust then top with chocolate candy pieces.*
9. *Place the pan back in the oven and bake for an additional 10-12 minutes or until firm to the touch.*
10. *Remove, let cool completely then cut into 14 thin bars and serve.*

MINI GERMAN PANCAKES

RECIPES

Makes 6 pancakes

Ingredients:

3/4 cup whole milk

3 eggs

3/4 cup all purpose flour

1/2 teaspoon kosher salt

6 teaspoons unsalted butter, cold

Apple or cherry pie filling, for serving

Powdered sugar, for serving

Method:

1. *Place the milk, eggs, flour and salt into a mixing bowl.*
2. *Attach the Wire Whisk to the Twist & Mix then set to the Whisk Position.*
3. *Whisk on HIGH for 2 minutes or until smooth and no lumps remain.*
4. *Preheat oven to 450°F with the oven rack in the bottom third of the oven.*
5. *Place a 6 spot muffin tin inside the oven and preheat for 5 minutes or until very hot.*
6. *Carefully add a teaspoon of butter into each well; let it melt for 5 minutes or until butter bubbles.*
7. *Using an oven mitt, pull out the oven rack halfway then carefully pour batter into the center of each well filling them 3/4 full; close oven.*
8. *Bake for 10-15 minutes or until dramatically puffed and brown.*
9. *Remove then spoon pie filling into the center of each mini pancake and dust with powdered sugar before serving.*

NO CHURN
ICE CREAM

Makes 6 cups

Ingredients:

2 cups heavy cream, cold
1 can (14 ounces) sweetened condensed milk
1/2 teaspoon vanilla extract
1/2 cup chocolate chips, divided
1/4 cup sprinkles, divided (optional)

Method:

1. *Pour the heavy cream into a mixing bowl.*
2. *Attach the Wire Whisk to the Twist & Mix then set to the Whisk Position.*
3. *Whisk on HIGH for 2 minutes or until thick.*
4. *Add the condensed milk and vanilla then whisk on LOW for 15 seconds to blend.*
5. *Pour 1/2 of the mixture into a freezer container.*
6. *Top with half of the chocolate chips and sprinkles then cover with remaining ice cream mixture before topping with remaining chocolate chips and sprinkles.*
7. *Cover and freeze for a minimum of 4 hours or until solid.*
8. *Serve frozen.*
9. *Ice cream can be kept in an airtight container in the freezer for up to 1 week.*

TIP

This makes wonderful vanilla ice cream if you omit the chocolate chips and sprinkles.

CORN
FRITTERS

Makes about 18 fritters

Ingredients:

3 large eggs yolks

2 tablespoons unsalted butter, melted

2 cups fresh or frozen yellow corn kernels

1 teaspoon vanilla extract

1/2 cup buttermilk

1/4 cup granulated sugar

1 1/2 cups all purpose flour

1 1/2 teaspoons kosher salt

2 teaspoons baking powder

2 large eggs

Oil, such as Canola, for frying

Powdered sugar, for dusting

Method:

1. *Place all ingredients, except oil and powdered sugar, into a mixing bowl.*
2. *Attach the Beater to the Twist & Mix then set to the Hand Mixer Position.*
3. *Beat on LOW for 10 seconds then increase speed to HIGH and beat for 30 seconds until thoroughly combined.*
4. *Heat 2-inches of oil in a large, heavy Dutch oven and heat to 350°F using a thermometer.*
5. *Carefully drop batter by the spoonfuls into the oil.*
6. *Fry for 2-4 minutes turning them over halfway until golden brown.*
7. *Remove and let drain on a wire rack set over absorbent paper on a sheet pan.*
8. *Repeat with remaining batter.*
9. *Dust with plenty of powdered sugar and serve hot.*

BOURSIN CHEESE
MASHED POTATOES

Makes 6 servings

Ingredients:

4 pounds Yukon Gold potatoes, peeled and chunked

Kosher salt and fresh pepper to taste

Cold water, as needed

1/4 cup unsalted butter

1 package (3 ounces) Boursin cheese

1 cup whole milk + more if needed

Method:

1. *Place potatoes and some salt into a large pot then add cold water until potatoes are covered by 1-inch of water.*
2. *Bring to a boil over high heat then reduce heat to a simmer.*
3. *Let potatoes simmer for 15 minutes or until tender.*
4. *Drain potatoes thoroughly.*
5. *Add more salt, pepper, butter and cheese to the potatoes.*
6. *Attach the Beater to the Twist & Mix then set to the Hand Mixer Position.*
7. *Mix potatoes on LOW then increase speed to HIGH while adding the milk.*
8. *Mix as quickly as possible for as short of time as possible until desired texture is achieved.*
9. *Garnish as desired and serve hot.*

TIP

Do not over mix the potatoes or they will become gluey instead of fluffy.

EGG WHITE OMELET

Makes 2 servings

Ingredients:

8 large egg whites

2 tablespoons feta cheese, crumbled

1/2 cup cooked broccoli, chopped

1/2 of a red bell pepper, sliced

Kosher salt and fresh pepper to taste

1 tablespoon olive oil

Method:

1. *Attach the Wire Whisk to the Twist & Mix then set to the Whisk Position.*
2. *Place egg whites into a large, narrow mixing bowl.*
3. *Whisk on HIGH for 2 minutes or until stiff peaks form.*
4. *Fold in remaining ingredients, except oil.*
5. *Preheat oil in a large skillet over medium heat and preheat oven broiler to LOW.*
6. *Pour the egg mixture into the skillet and cook for 2 minutes undisturbed.*
7. *After 2 minutes, place skillet under the broiler and cook for an additional 2-3 minutes or until browned, puffy and just set.*
8. *Remove, garnish as desired and serve immediately.*

HOMEMADE RANCH
DRESSING

Makes about 4 cups

Ingredients:

1 cup Homemade Mayonnaise (see page 100)

1 cup sour cream

1 1/2 teaspoons onion powder

3/4 teaspoon dried chives

3/4 teaspoon dried parsley

3/4 teaspoon garlic powder

3/4 teaspoon Kosher salt

1/2 teaspoon freshly ground pepper

1/2 teaspoon dried oregano, ground

2 cups buttermilk

Method:

1. *Place all ingredients into a mixing bowl.*
2. *Attach the Beater to the Twist & Mix then set to the Hand Mixer Position.*
3. *Beat on LOW for 1 minute or until combined.*
4. *Dressing can be kept in an airtight container in the refrigerator for up to 1 week.*

SAVORY BREAD
PUDDING

Makes 6 servings

Ingredients:

6 large croissants, chunked

1 small yellow onion, chopped

1 medium tomato, chopped

1 cup fresh spinach, torn

1 cup kielbasa sausage, sliced

6 large eggs

1 1/2 cups half & half

Kosher salt and fresh pepper to taste

1 tablespoon red wine vinegar

1 cup Parmesan cheese, grated

Method:

1. Preheat oven to 375°F and apply nonstick cooking spray to a 9x13-inch baking dish.
2. Scatter the croissants, onions, tomatoes, spinach and kielbasa across the bottom of the baking dish; set aside.
3. Place remaining ingredients into a large mixing bowl.
4. Attach the Wire Whisk to the Twist & Mix then set to the Whisk Position.
5. Whisk mixing bowl contents on HIGH for 1 minute or until well mixed.
6. Pour mixture over baking dish contents then press down to help the bread absorb the mixture.
7. Bake for 30-40 minutes or until puffed and well browned.
8. Garnish as desired and serve hot.

TIP

This recipe can easily be altered to use ingredients you already have in your refrigerator. You can use most meats (or no meat) and almost any leftover vegetable you find tasty.

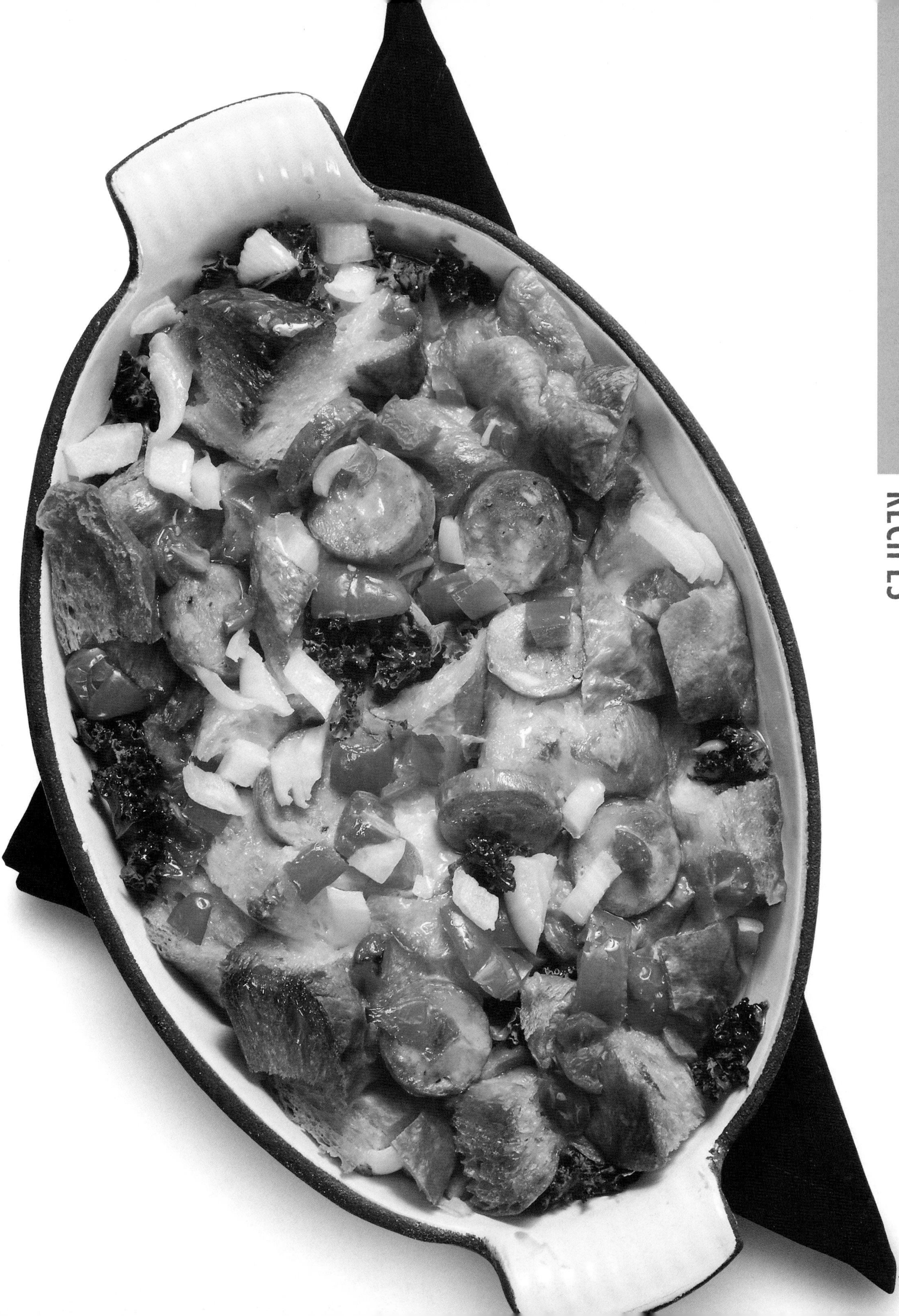

VEGAN (EGGLESS) MAYONNAISE

Makes about 1 1/2 cups

Ingredients:

4 tablespoons aquafaba (the liquid from a 15.5 ounce can of chickpeas)
1 teaspoon dry mustard powder
1/2 to 1 teaspoon kosher salt or to taste
2 teaspoons fresh lemon juice
1 cup canola or other neutral-flavored oil

Method:

1. *Place all ingredients into a canning jar or storage container.*
2. *Attach the Drink Mixer to the Twist & Mix then set to the Drink Mixer Position.*
3. *Position the Drink Mixer attachment at bottom of the container then turn speed to HIGH.*
4. *Mix ingredients on HIGH for 30 seconds to start emulsifying, keeping the Drink Mixer attachment at the bottom of the container.*
5. *Slowly raise mixer up until a thick mayonnaise forms.*
6. *Mayonnaise can be kept in an airtight container in the refrigerator for up to 1 week.*

TIP

This mayonnaise tastes just like regular mayo but since it does not contain egg it is perfect for picnics or outdoor entertaining.

EGG
FOO YONG

Makes 4 servings

Ingredients:

6 large eggs

6 garlic cloves, minced

1 tablespoon fresh ginger, minced

1 bunch green onions, sliced

3 tablespoons bottled soy sauce

1 tablespoon dark sesame oil

3 tablespoons corn starch

1 large yellow onion, sliced

1/2 red bell pepper, sliced

1/2 head green cabbage, thinly sliced

8 ounces small shrimp, peeled and deveined

Canola oil, for the griddle

Method:

1. *Place the eggs, garlic, ginger, green onions, soy sauce, sesame oil and corn starch into a large bowl.*
2. *Attach the Beater to the Twist & Mix then set to the Hand Mixer Position.*
3. *Mix on HIGH for 1 minute or until thoroughly mixed.*
4. *Using a spoon, stir in the onions, bell peppers, cabbage and shrimp.*
5. *Preheat a griddle pan to medium-high heat.*
6. *Lightly oil the griddle.*
7. *Using a cooking spoon, ladle a few mounds of mixture onto griddle and pat down slightly.*
8. *Cook for 3-4 minutes on each side or until well browned.*
9. *Remove and repeat with remaining mixture.*
10. *Garnish as desired and serve.*

RASPBERRY SAUCE

Makes 2 cups

Ingredients:

1 bag (12 ounces) frozen raspberries, thawed
1 cup granulated sugar

Method:

1. *Place all ingredients into a tall narrow container.*
2. *Attach the Drink Mixer to the Twist & Mix then set to the Drink Mixer Position.*
3. *Mix on HIGH for 1-2 minutes or until raspberries are broken down.*
4. *Use as desired.*

TIP

You can substitute blackberries for the raspberries. This sauce also freezes well for up to 3 months.

PINEAPPLE UPSIDE DOWN CAKE

Makes 1 cake

Ingredients:

For the Pan:

3 tablespoons unsalted butter, softened

4 tablespoons light brown sugar, packed

1 can (17 ounces) pineapple slices

Maraschino cherries, no stems, as needed for center of pineapples

For the Batter:

2/3 cup granulated sugar

1/4 cup unsalted butter, softened

1 large egg

2/3 cup pineapple juice

2 teaspoons vanilla extract

2 teaspoons baking powder

1 1/3 cups unbleached all purpose flour

Method:

1. *Preheat oven to 350°F.*
2. *Grease the bottom and sides of an 8-inch cake pan with 3 tablespoons of butter.*
3. *Sprinkle brown sugar across the pan then twirl pan until the butter is evenly coated with sugar.*
4. *Press the pineapple slices evenly across the bottom of the pan into the butter.*
5. *Press a cherry into the center of each pineapple slice.*
6. *Place all batter ingredients into a mixing bowl.*
7. *Attach the Beater to the Twist & Mix then set to the Hand Mixer Position.*
8. *Mix on LOW for 30 seconds then increase speed to HIGH and mix for 1-2 minutes until combined.*
9. *Pour the batter into the pineapple-lined pan and smooth out the top using a rubber spatula.*
10. *Bake for 25-30 minutes; to test for doneness insert a wooden pick off-center, it should come out with just a few moist crumbs clinging to it.*
11. *Let cool for 10 minutes then loosen the edge with a table knife and invert the cake onto a serving plate.*

RUM PUNCH IN A WATERMELON

Makes 6-8 servings

Ingredients:

1 small watermelon
Juice of 1 lime
1/4 cup powdered sugar
Rum, to taste

Method:

1. *Using a large knife, trim off the bottom (horizontally) from the long side of the melon. This will stabilize the watermelon and prevent it from rolling.*
2. *Cut a square opening into the top center of the watermelon; reserve the square as it will serve as a plug later.*
3. *Attach the Beater to the Twist & Mix then set to the Drink Mixer Position.*
4. *Push the beater as far down into the melon flesh as possible.*
5. *Start mixing on LOW then gently move Twist & Mix around for 3-4 minutes or until watermelon is completely broken up into a pulpy juice.*
6. *Finish mixing on HIGH for 1 minute.*
7. *If watermelon is very full, pour off about 1-2 cups of juice and reserve for another use.*
8. *Add remaining ingredients into the watermelon opening then mix again on LOW just until blended.*
9. *Insert the reserved square plug that you cut out in step 2 then refrigerate for a few hours or overnight.*
10. *Serve with straws.*

TIP

For a non-alcoholic version, omit the rum and increase the limes to 2 and up the powdered sugar to 1/2 cup.

WOLF'S LEMON BARS

Makes about 16 bars

Ingredients:

For the Crust:

1 1/2 cups all purpose flour

1 tablespoon lemon zest

1/4 cup powdered sugar

1/2 cup unsalted butter, melted

For the Lemon Filling:

4 eggs

1 1/4 cups sugar

2 tablespoons all purpose flour

2 tablespoons lemon zest

1/2 cup fresh lemon juice

1/2 teaspoon kosher salt

1/2 teaspoon vanilla extract

Powdered sugar, for dusting

Method:

1. Preheat oven to 350°F.
2. In a bowl, combine all crust ingredients; mix using a fork until a crumbly dough forms.
3. Press the dough into the bottom of a greased 9x9-inch baking pan.
4. Bake for 15-20 minutes or until light golden brown.
5. Place all filling ingredients, except powdered sugar, into a mixing bowl.
6. Attach the Beater to the Twist & Mix then set to the Hand Mixer Position.
7. Mix on LOW for 30 seconds then increase speed to HIGH and mix for 3-4 minutes or until thick.
8. Pour filling over the hot crust.
9. Place the baking pan back in the oven and bake for an additional 20-25 minutes or until the filling is firm to the touch.
10. Remove, let cool completely then cut into squares.
11. Dust with powdered sugar before serving.

TIP

Turn these into lime or grapefruit bars by substituting the juice and zest.

PEANUT BUTTER
PIE

Makes 1 pie

Ingredients:

1 package (8 ounces) cream cheese, softened

4 ounces unsalted butter

1 cup powdered sugar

1 cup creamy peanut butter

1/2 teaspoon vanilla extract

1 store-bought chocolate cookie pie crust

Old Fashioned Whipped Cream, for topping (see page 24)

Roasted peanuts, for serving

Method:

1. *Place all ingredients, except pie crust, whipped cream and peanuts, into a mixing bowl.*
2. *Attach the Beater to the Twist & Mix then set to the Hand Mixer Position.*
3. *Mix on LOW for 1-2 minutes or until smooth.*
4. *Pour mixture into the pie crust and refrigerate for 1-2 hours or until firm.*
5. *Top with whipped cream and peanuts then garnish as desired and serve.*

NO ROLL BISCUITS

Makes 12 biscuits

Ingredients:

1 1/2 cups all purpose flour
1 tablespoon granulated sugar
2 1/4 teaspoons baking powder
1/2 teaspoon kosher salt
1 cup heavy cream
Additional heavy cream and sugar, for tops

Method:

1. *Preheat oven to 375°F and line a cookie sheet with parchment paper.*
2. *Place all ingredients into a mixing bowl.*
3. *Attach the Beater to the Twist & Mix then set to the Hand Mixer Position.*
4. *Mix on LOW then increase speed to HIGH and mix for 1 minute or until a rough dough ball forms.*
5. *Using a small ice cream scoop, drop biscuits onto prepared cookie sheet then pat down tops using your fingers.*
6. *Brush each biscuit with some additional cream then sprinkle with additional sugar.*
7. *Bake for 15-17 minutes or until golden brown and puffed.*
8. *Remove and serve hot.*

TIP

The raw biscuit dough freezes beautifully. Scoop dough onto a parchment-lined cookie sheet and freeze the mounds of dough until solid. Transfer to a zipper-top bag and freeze for up to 1 month. Bake biscuits from a frozen state at the same temperature adding 5 minutes to the baking time.

BUTTER PECAN
MILKSHAKE

Makes 1 serving

Ingredients:

4 big scoops vanilla ice cream

1/2 teaspoon vanilla butter & nut extract

1/2 cup whole milk

1/4 cup toasted pecans, chopped + more for topping

Method:

1. *Place all ingredients into a tall drinking glass.*
2. *Attach the Drink Mixer to the Twist & Mix then set to the Drink Mixer Position.*
3. *Mix on LOW for a few seconds then increase speed to HIGH until smooth.*
4. *Top with additional chopped pecans, garnish as desired and serve immediately.*

CRISPY BANANA
BEIGNETS

Makes 4-6 servings

Ingredients:

2 cups complete buttermilk pancake mix

2 cups whole milk, cold

1/4 cup granulated sugar

1/2 teaspoon vanilla extract

Oil, such as canola, for frying

3 ripe bananas, sliced

Powdered sugar, for serving

Method:

1. *Place the pancake mix, milk, sugar and vanilla into a narrow mixing bowl.*
2. *Attach the Wire Whisk to the Twist & Mix then set to the Whisk Position.*
3. *Whisk on LOW for 30 seconds or until batter is fairly smooth with a few lumps.*
4. *In a large, heavy Dutch oven, heat 2-inches of oil to 350°F using a thermometer.*
5. *Dip a few banana slices into the batter then add to the oil.*
6. *Fry for 2 minutes on each side or until browned and crispy.*
7. *Remove, drain on absorbent paper then repeat with remaining banana slices.*
8. *Dust with powdered sugar and serve immediately.*

VEGGIE OMELET

Makes 2 servings

Ingredients:

6 large eggs

1 cup spinach, chopped

1/2 cup mushrooms, chopped

1 green onion, sliced

Kosher salt and fresh pepper to taste

8 small grape tomatoes, sliced

1/4 cup Parmesan cheese, grated

1 tablespoon olive oil

Method:

1. *Place all ingredients, except oil, into a large narrow mixing bowl.*
2. *Attach the Wire Whisk to the Twist & Mix then set to the Whisk Position.*
3. *Whisk on HIGH for 2 minutes or until well blended and foamy.*
4. *Preheat the oil in a large skillet over medium heat and preheat oven broiler to LOW.*
5. *Pour the egg mixture into the skillet and cook for 2 minutes undisturbed.*
6. *Place skillet under broiler and cook for an additional 2-3 minutes or until browned, puffy and just set.*
7. *Remove, garnish as desired and serve immediately.*

EASY
SNICKERDOODLES

Makes 3-4 dozen Snickerdoodles

Ingredients:

1/2 cup unsalted butter, softened

1/2 cup shortening

1 1/2 cups granulated sugar

2 large eggs

2 teaspoons vanilla extract

2 3/4 cups all purpose flour

2 teaspoons cream of tartar

1 teaspoon baking soda

1/4 teaspoon kosher salt

Cinnamon sugar, for rolling

Method:

1. Preheat oven to 400°F and line cookie sheets with parchment paper; set aside.
2. Place butter, shortening, sugar, eggs and vanilla into a large mixing bowl.
3. Attach the Beater to the Twist & Mix then set to the Hand Mixer Position.
4. Mix on LOW then increase speed to HIGH and mix for 2-3 minutes or until well creamed.
5. Reduce speed to LOW then blend in the flour, cream of tartar, baking soda and salt.
6. Shape dough by rounded spoonfuls into balls.
7. Roll balls in cinnamon sugar to coat then place on prepared cookie sheets.
8. Bake in batches for 8 minutes or until puffed but pale in color.
9. Remove and let cool before serving.

SALTED CARAMEL
PARTY DIP

Makes 3 cups

Ingredients:

2 packages (8 ounces each) cream cheese, softened

1/4 cup unsalted butter, softened

1/2 cup jarred caramel sauce

1/2 teaspoon vanilla extract

Kosher salt

Cookies, for dipping

Method:

1. *Place cream cheese, butter, caramel, vanilla and a pinch of salt into a mixing bowl.*
2. *Attach the Beater to the Twist & Mix then set to the Hand Mixer Position.*
3. *Mix on LOW then increase speed to HIGH and mix for 1-2 minutes or until smooth.*
4. *Scoop into a serving dish then sprinkle with additional salt.*
5. *Serve with cookies for dipping.*

WOLF'S BREAD
PUDDING

Makes 6 servings

Ingredients:

6 large croissants, cut into chunks

1 1/2 cups heavy cream

4 large eggs

1/2 cup granulated sugar + more for topping

Pinch of kosher salt

2 teaspoons fresh lemon juice

1 teaspoon vanilla extract

1/2 ripe banana, sliced

1 cup fresh or frozen berries

1/2 cup white, dark or mixed chocolate chips

Method:

1. *Preheat oven to 375°F.*
2. *Place croissants into a greased 8x8-inch baking pan.*
3. *Place remaining ingredients, except bananas, berries and chocolate chips, into a mixing bowl.*
4. *Attach the Wire Whisk to the Twist & Mix then set to the Whisk Position.*
5. *Mix on LOW for 1-2 minutes until combined.*
6. *Pour mixture over the baking pan contents.*
7. *Scatter banana slices, berries and chocolate chips over the top then sprinkle with additional sugar.*
8. *Bake for 30-40 minutes or until browned and firm to the touch.*
9. *Remove, garnish as desired and serve warm.*

TIP

The Old Fashioned Whipped Cream on page 24 is excellent with this bread pudding.

SPINACH ARTICHOKE
QUESADILLA

Makes 1 quesadilla

Ingredients:

3 ounces cream cheese, softened

2 ounces jarred artichoke hearts

1 cup fresh spinach leaves, julienned

1/4 cup mozzarella cheese, grated

Kosher salt and fresh pepper to taste

2 large flour tortillas

1 tablespoon olive oil

Method:

1. *Place all ingredients, except tortillas and oil, into a mixing bowl.*
2. *Attach the Beater to the Twist & Mix then set to the Hand Mixer Position.*
3. *Mix on LOW for 1 minute or until well blended.*
4. *Spread mixture over one of the tortillas.*
5. *Top with the second tortilla.*
6. *Preheat the oil in a large sauté pan over medium heat.*
7. *Place the quesadilla into the sauté pan and cook for 2 minutes on each side or until brown.*
8. *Remove, cut into wedges, garnish as desired and serve.*

TIP

Use this recipe as a template and add or subtract ingredients as you like. Just remember to use some sort of cheese as it acts like a glue to keep it from falling apart.

JUICY SHREDDED
CHICKEN BREASTS

Makes 6-8 servings

Ingredients:

6 boneless, skinless chicken breasts

3 tablespoons chicken-flavored bouillon base or to taste

Kosher salt and fresh pepper to taste

4 garlic cloves, left whole

1 large yellow onion, chopped

1 bay leaf

3 cups water

Method:

1. *Preheat oven to 350°F.*
2. *Place all ingredients into a large Dutch oven; stir then cover tightly.*
3. *Bake for 3 hours or until chicken is very tender.*
4. *Remove and let cool for 15 minutes then drain off and reserve the juices from the Dutch oven. Discard bay leaf.*
5. *Attach the Beater to the Twist & Mix then set to the Hand Mixer Position.*
6. *Use your Twist & Mix on LOW to break up and shred the chicken.*
7. *When thoroughly shredded, return the reserved juices to the chicken.*
8. *Garnish as desired and serve.*

TIP

These can be cooked in 8 minutes using a pressure cooker if you are pressed for time.

CHEESE
SOUFFLÉ

Makes 4 servings

Ingredients:

1/3 cup Parmesan cheese, grated and divided

4 large eggs

1 cup Gruyere cheese, shredded

1/4 cup sour cream

1/3 cup whole milk

1/2 teaspoon dry mustard

1/4 teaspoon kosher salt

1/8 teaspoon freshly ground black pepper

2 tablespoons fresh parsley, minced

1 tablespoon fresh chives, minced

2 tablespoons all purpose flour

Method:

1. *Preheat oven to 350°F.*

2. *Lightly apply nonstick cooking spray to the bottom and sides of four soufflé dishes.*

3. *Sprinkle the soufflé dishes with 2 tablespoons of Parmesan cheese then place on a baking sheet.*

4. *Place remaining ingredients into a mixing bowl.*

5. *Attach the Beater to the Twist & Mix then set to the Hand Mixer Position.*

6. *Beat on HIGH for 1-2 minutes or until thoroughly combined.*

7. *Pour mixture into prepared soufflé dishes until 1/2-inch from the top edge of dish.*

8. *Bake in center of the oven for 30 minutes or until puffed and brown.*

9. *Remove, garnish as desired and serve immediately.*

HOMEMADE
MAYONNAISE

Makes about 1 3/4 cups

Ingredients:

2 pasteurized large eggs

1 tablespoon Dijon mustard

2 tablespoons fresh lemon juice

1 teaspoon Kosher salt or to taste

1 1/2 cups grapeseed or canola oil, divided

Method:

1. *Place all ingredients, except oil, into a tall, narrow container or a canning jar.*
2. *Attach the Wire Whisk to the Twist & Mix then set to the Whisk Position.*
3. *Whisk on HIGH for 30 seconds to blend thoroughly.*
4. *While continuing to whisk on HIGH, slowly start to stream 3/4 cup of oil into the container then start to add remaining oil faster as you see the mayonnaise take shape (it should take about 1 minute to add all of the oil).*
5. *Mayonnaise can be kept in an airtight container in the refrigerator for up to 1 week.*

SPAGHETTI BAKE

Makes 4 servings

Ingredients:

8 ounces cream cheese, softened

1 cup Parmesan cheese, grated

2 large eggs

Kosher salt and fresh pepper to taste

2 cups pasta sauce

2 teaspoons garlic powder

2 cups mozzarella cheese, grated

1 pound spaghetti noodles, cooked

Method:

1. *Preheat oven to 350°F then apply nonstick cooking spray to an 8x8-inch baking dish.*
2. *Place cream cheese, Parmesan, eggs, salt and pepper into a large mixing bowl.*
3. *Attach the Beater to the Twist & Mix then set to the Hand Mixer Position.*
4. *Mix on LOW then increase speed to HIGH and mix for 1 minute or until blended.*
5. *While mixing on LOW, add the pasta sauce, garlic and mozzarella until blended.*
6. *Add the noodles, mix using a spatula until combined then scrape into the prepared baking dish.*
7. *Bake for 30-40 minutes or until brown and bubbly.*
8. *Remove, garnish as desired and serve hot.*

VANILLA SHEET CAKE

Makes 1 cake

Ingredients:

1 3/4 cups granulated sugar

1/2 cup unsalted butter, softened

1/2 cup solid white shortening

1 teaspoon kosher salt

1 tablespoon baking powder

1 teaspoon vanilla extract

1/4 teaspoon butter vanilla extract

1/8 teaspoon almond extract

5 large egg whites

2 3/4 cups cake flour

1 cup whole milk

Method:

1. Preheat oven to 350°F.
2. Butter and flour a 9x13-inch baking pan then set aside.
3. Place the sugar, butter, shortening, salt and baking powder into a mixing bowl.
4. Attach the Beater to the Twist & Mix then set to the Hand Mixer Position.
5. Beat on LOW for 5 minutes then scrape down the bowl using a spatula.
6. Mix in the extracts and egg whites on LOW.
7. Add the flour and milk in batches using LOW speed until all is added and batter is uniform in color; don't over mix.
8. Pour batter into prepared 9x13-inch baking pan.
9. Bake for 20-25 minutes; to test for doneness insert a wooden pick off-center, it should come out with just a few moist crumbs clinging to it.
10. Let cool for 10 minutes before removing from pan.

TIP

To ice the cake as shown in the picture, make the Old Fashioned Whipped Cream on page 24 then briefly stir in 1/2 cup store-bought chocolate sauce until streaky.

LEMONADE FREEZER PIE

Makes one 8-inch pie

Ingredients:

1 package (3 ounces) lemon-flavored gelatin

1/2 cup granulated sugar

1/2 cup boiling water

3 packages (8 ounces each) cream cheese, very soft

Juice and zest of 1 lemon + more for topping

1 store-bought graham cracker pie crust

Old Fashioned Whipped Cream (see page 24)

RECIPES

Method:

1. *Pour the gelatin, sugar and boiling water into a large mixing bowl and stir to dissolve.*
2. *Add the cream cheese, lemon juice and zest.*
3. *Attach the Beater to the Twist & Mix then set to the Hand Mixer Position.*
4. *Mix on LOW then increase speed to HIGH and mix for 2 minutes or until smooth.*
5. *Pour into pie crust and freeze for 1 hour or until cold and set.*
6. *Cover with Old Fashioned Whipped Cream then top with additional lemon zest and slices.*
7. *Serve cold.*

VANILLA
MILKSHAKE

Makes 1 serving

Ingredients:

4 big scoops vanilla ice cream
1/2 teaspoon vanilla extract
1/2 cup whole milk

Method:

1. *Place all ingredients into a tall drinking glass.*
2. *Attach the Drink Mixer to the Twist & Mix then set to the Drink Mixer Position.*
3. *Mix on LOW then increase speed to HIGH and mix until smooth.*
4. *Garnish as desired and serve immediately.*

OATMEAL COOKIES

Makes about 36 cookies

Ingredients:

1 3/4 cups unsalted butter, softened
1 cup granulated sugar
1 cup light brown sugar, packed
2 large eggs
1 teaspoon vanilla extract
1/2 teaspoon kosher salt
1 1/4 cups raisins
1 teaspoon baking soda
1 1/2 cups all purpose flour
3 cups old fashioned rolled oats

Method:

1. Preheat oven to 350°F.
2. Line a cookie sheet with parchment paper.
3. Place butter and both sugars into a mixing bowl.
4. Attach the Beater to the Twist & Mix then set to the Hand Mixer Position.
5. Beat on LOW for 1-2 minutes or until fluffy.
6. Add the eggs, vanilla and salt then beat on LOW while adding remaining ingredients; mix until combined.
7. Using an ice cream scoop, drop even scoops of batter 2-inches apart onto the prepared cookie sheet.
8. Bake for 12-15 minutes or until golden brown and slightly puffy.
9. Remove then repeat with remaining dough and serve warm.

TIP

These cookies can be stored in an airtight container at room temperature for up to 3 days.

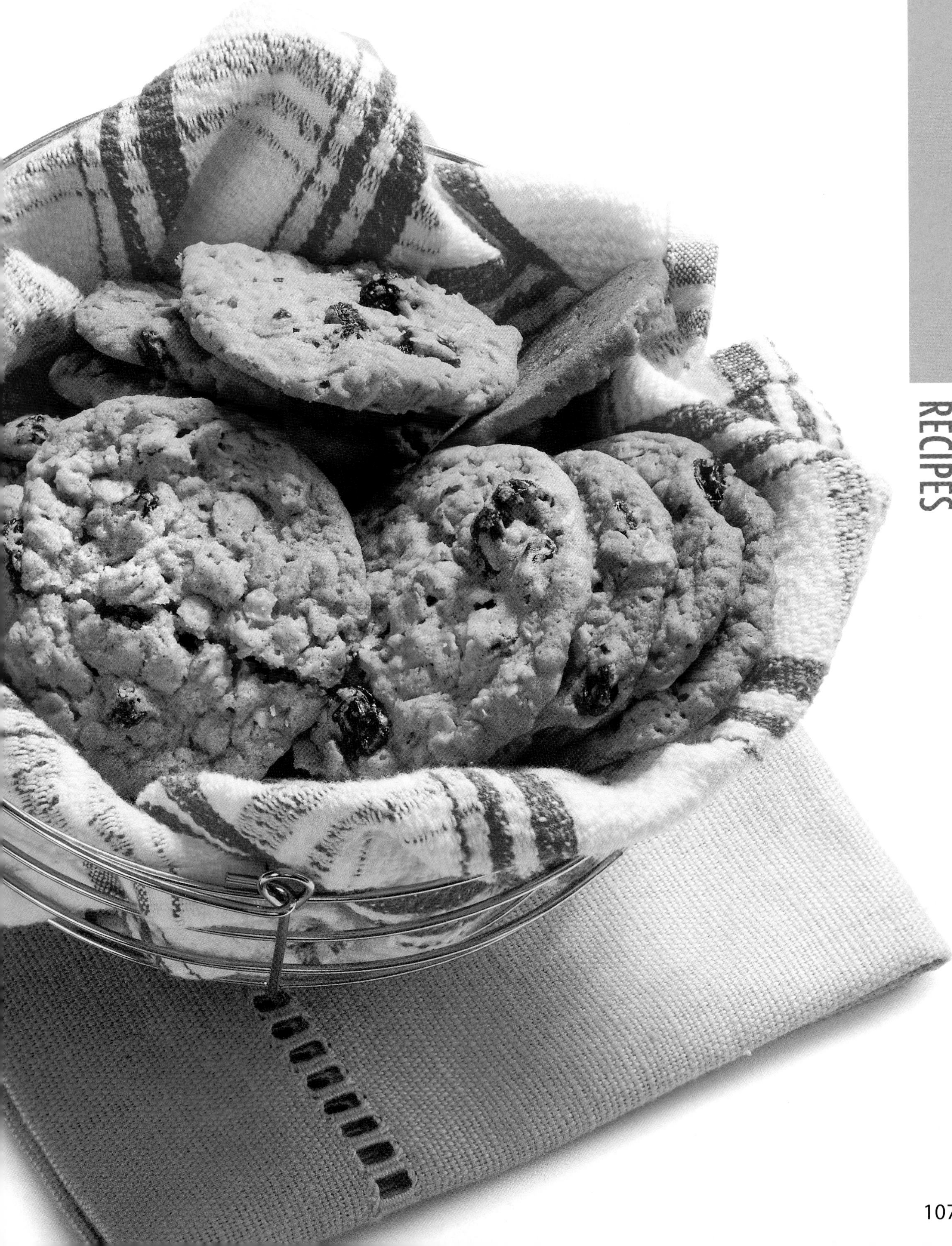

SOURCE PAGE

Here are some of my favorite places to find ingredients that are not readily available at grocery stores as well as kitchen tools and supplies that help you become a better cook.

The Bakers Catalogue at King Arthur Flour

135 Route 5 South
P.O. Box 1010
Norwich, VT 05055

Flours, pure fruit oils, citric acid, baker's ammonia, blow torches, kitchen tools, baking pans
www.kingarthurflour.com

Rolling Pin Kitchen Emporium

P.O. Box 21798
Long Beach, CA 90801
customerservice@rollingpin.com

Baker's ammonia, cheesecloths, kitchen tools
www.rollingpin.com

Chocosphere

P.O. Box 2237
Tualatin, OR 97062
877-992-4623

Excellent quality cocoa (Callebaut)
All Chocolates
Jimmies and sprinkles
www.chocosphere.com

Gluten Free Mall

4927 Sonoma HWY Suite C1
Santa Rosa, CA 95409
707-509-4528

All ingredients needed for gluten-free baking
www.glutenfreemall.com

Vanilla From Tahiti

Nui Enterprises
501 Chapala St. Suite A
Santa Barbara, CA 93101
805-965-5153

pure vanilla extracts and high quality vanilla beans
www.vanillafromtahiti.com

D & G Occasions

625 Herndon Ave.
Orlando, FL 32803
407-894-4458

My favorite butter vanilla extract by Magic Line, cake and candy making supplies, citric acid, pure fruit oils, professional food colorings, ultra thin flexible spatulas, large selection of sprinkles and jimmies, unusual birthday candles, pure vanilla extract, pastry bags and tips, parchment, off-set spatulas, oven and candy thermometers, silicone shot glass mold pans, large selection of cookie cutters
www.dandgoccasions.com

Penzeys Spices

P.O. Box 924
Brookfield, WI 53045
800-741-7787

Spices, extracts, seasonings, and more
www.penzeys.com

Whole Foods

550 Bowie St.
Austin, TX 78703
(512) 499-4455

grains, citric acid, natural and organic products, xanthan gum, gluten-free baking items
www.wholefoodsmarket.com

FOR ALL OF MARIAN GETZ'S
COOKBOOKS AS WELL AS
COOKWARE, APPLIANCES, CUTLERY
AND KITCHEN ACCESSORIES
BY WOLFGANG PUCK

PLEASE VISIT
HSN.COM
(KEYWORD: WOLFGANG PUCK)